Dormie One: And Other Golf Stories

Holworthy Hall, Century Company

DORMIE ONE

AND OTHER GOLF STORIES

He went forward, elucidating the caddy's pedigree to him as he went

DORMIE ONE
AND OTHER GOLF STORIES

BY

HOLWORTHY HALL

Author of "My Next Imitation," "Henry of Navarre,
Ohio," "Pepper," "Paprika," "Help Wanted,"
"What He Least Expected," etc.

NEW YORK
THE CENTURY CO.
1917

\

T

TO

THE FINEST SPORTSMAN
THE KINDEST TUTOR
AND THE BEST GOLFING COMPANION
OF MY ACQUAINTANCE

GRANTLAND RICE

THIS BOOK IS
AFFECTIONATELY DEDICATED

A RAMBLING PREFACE

(Of No Particular Interest to Any One but the Author)

The game of golf is of ancient origin — ancient far beyond the dogmas of any sporting historian. Virgil, in the second book of the Georgics, wrote: "*Miscueruntque herbas, et non innoxia verba,*" which, being liberally translated, means: "And they stood in the rough, and cursed." Herodotus, evidently mindful of one of the sections of Rule XXVIII, once said: "*Akineta kineis,*" or "You're smoothing the line of your putt, and it's my hole." Mr. George Herbert, in his "Outlandish Proverbs," published in 1639, stated flatly that "he who once hits is ever bending"; and John Ray, writing a century later, quoted as a very aged and bewhiskered motto: "Youth will have its swing." And of course if I chose to adduce scriptural evidence to demonstrate that long tee-shots are not entirely the result of rubber-cored balls, I could easily refer to II Kings, ix, 20, wherein the discourse is of the driving of Jehu, the son of Nimshi, "for he driveth furiously."

A RAMBLING PREFACE

But it was in England, during the Victorian Era, that golf became at once a cure and a disease; and its regeneration was chiefly due to the exigencies of the age. Not to be contented is one of the greatest privileges of mankind; and the Victorian Era was typified by a national lack of this blessing. England, comparatively free from the civic stimulant of wars and riots, was wallowing in the sybaritic sweetness of supercomplacency, and golf appeared as a welcome antidote, because golf alone could provide that ingredient of agonized despair which is the safeguard of every progressive community. Nobody who plays golf can maintain a set standard of contentment; even if one is on one's game, one's opponent is likely to have all the luck, or there's a slow foursome ahead, or the greens are too keen, or not keen enough, or something. It is rare indeed that the world contains a player who is wholly, utterly, absolutely satisfied with his last round, or his best round, or any round. Read Owen Johnson's " Even Threes."

In America, that Newport tournament of 1893 was a prophylaxis. It saved us from possible Victorianism of our own; it inaugurated the first of our local anthropological periods, that division of the calendar which might be characterized as the Quaternary, or Flinty, or Van Cortlandt period, when

the words "tee" and "caddy," if judiciously combined, were supposed to constitute a side-splitting
joke, and a red coat was more than half the battle.
Thence we proceeded through the mesolithic, and
neolithic (or aluminum) period, emerged into the
iron age and the Nassau system of finance, and came
presently, after the lingering death of Colonel Bogey, to the modern, or Christian era, which has
stamped Donald Ross as the supreme architect of
golf courses, and permitted us to leave our foot-
prints in more sands than Longfellow ever imagined.

But despite the probability that all the golfers of
America, if placed end to end — never mind; I shall
leave the mathematics to some one else — despite
the vast number of golfers in America, the literature
of the game has been almost exclusively technical.
Sutphen and Spearman, Sabin, Johnson, Morris,
Van Loan and Tillinghast — and the fiction of golf
is only seven up, with eleven still to go. Generous
bibliographies of other sports might readily be com-
piled, but golf in fiction remains in the status of
golf in fact two decades ago. This is not fair;
and rather than write letters to the "Times" about
it, I have tried the obvious alternative.

But golf is a difficult game in which to immor-
talize a hero. "The Maltese Cat" is one thing,

and Lamar's run and Charlie Brickley's field goals
and Ty Cobb's batting and Maurice McLoughlin's
tennis are other things; golf is comparatively aca-
demic, and almost entirely subjective. Furthermore, it fails in romantic variety of situations.
Take a good newspaper account of the Harvard-
Yale football game, or of the Jeffries-Johnson fight,
and place it alongside the finest available description of Francis Ouimet's round against Ray and
Vardon, and the episode at Brookline runs like the
report of a professional surveyor chasing a couple
of moths without the use of triangulation. The
terminology of golf is stunted; there are too few
expressions to cover the too few incidents. It is
conceivable to depict Sam White's touchdown in a
thousand ways; but in how many different sentences can you describe the sinking of a short putt?

Then, too, the inexorable routine of a match
is confining; there are eighteen or thirty-six
holes to play, and a writer is constantly falling
back on his arithmetic. And it hurts. In the
gridiron story, your hero can spend five hundred
words, if necessary, in dodging two tacklers and
giving the straight-arm to a third; in golf, the hero
is invariably driving a precise distance (or the
reader wouldn't believe it was a good drive), playing a second shot of a hundred and eighty-six

yards, two feet, and seven inches (or the critic would have no basis of judgment) and placing his brilliant approach within nineteen millimeters of the hole. I know of only one other sport which offers fewer possibilities for a red-blooded story of nerve and skill and stamina — and that 's billiards!

I have played golf for more than twenty years, and I know all the hard-luck stories there are. I have seen all the possible flukes, and some that I knew were impossible even after I saw them. With my own eyes I have watched a 40 handicap man tie for the net prize in a medal play — by getting a *one* on the last hole. I have seen a very excellent tournament player lose a match after being 6 up with 7 to go. I have partnered a novice who suddenly scored an 84 on a full-length course, and immediately dropped back to his former average of 104. I have seen one of the best golfers in America stoop confidently to make a six-foot putt for a par 3, and eventually go down in 8. I was present on the occasion when a state champion made a clean foozle of a putt — the club never touched the ball. I have seen a man get two hundred yards with a brassey out of the limbs of an apple-tree; and I have seen an old Haskell ball impaled so firmly on a barb of a wire fence that since the wind was blowing strongly, the ball was alternately within the course, and out of bounds. And I played in the Kickers' tournament, some years ago, in which the winner had awarded himself a handicap of 60, and played under a hundred. With those incidents standing as realities, where are the boundary lines of fiction?

There are two stories in this volume which seem to demand some slight explanation. "Dormie One" is the first. I have received many letters and many verbal communications in regard to it, and I have to say in reply that never in my life have I set eyes on the famous veteran who, in the opinion of some of his friends, has been portrayed; nor did I intend to represent or even to suggest him. The story is purely imaginative; it has no substratum of truth whatsoever.

The second story is "The Luck of the Devil." I have been warned that it appears to parallel in construction, but not in subject-matter, a certain conte of Leonard Merrick's. Well, it ought to. I was under the positive influence of Merrick when I wrote it.

All eight narratives reflect, naturally, many years of golf and many years of association with golfers. The good players used to avoid me; now they bring me plots. The bad players have helped to make me resigned to fate; and they still criticize my

xii

* Perhaps not, but see Jerome D. Travers, "The Winning Shot" (true golf stories) ny. Doubleday, 1915, p. 63-66 technique. Both classes have been of invaluable assistance, and I hereby acknowledge my debt to those who have directly and indirectly contributed to my store of golf anecdotes, and enlarged my treasury of golfing notes.

Tom Hucknall, sometime professional, Kearsarge Golf Club, New Hampshire. C. W. Singleton, professional at Siwanoy, 1915. Donald Ross, Pinehurst, 1917.

Charles W. Corbett, F. L. E. Gauss, C. A. Speakman, J. C. Scobie, John F. Woods and Robert A. Tinsman, of the Siwanoy Golf Club.

Don M. Parker, Garden City; Grantland Rice, Englewood; Lee Maxwell, Sleepy Hollow; Gardner W. White, Flushing; Charles M. Morton, Forest Hill F. C.; John Balmer, Yountakah; Leslie A. Gillette, Salisbury; H. R. Reed, Knickerbocker; Francis X. Barr, Exmoor; Roy S. Durstine, Scarsdale; Julian E. Garnsey, Gedney Farm; Bradford S. Turpin, Woodland; Leslie E. Kreider, Westfield; Douglas Z. Doty and Frederick Dorr Steele.

CONTENTS

	PAGE
ALIBI	3
IF YOU DON'T MIND MY TELLING YOU . . .	48
THE RUNNER-UP	95
THE LUCK OF THE DEVIL	141
THE LAST ROUND	186
IF IT INTERFERES WITH BUSINESS	229
DORMIE ONE	271
"CONSOLATION"	307

LIST OF ILLUSTRATIONS

PAGE

He went forward, elucidating the caddy's pedigree to him as he went . . . . *Frontispiece*

But to-day he looked mercilessly upon the scoundrel, and saw him for what he was, a trafficker in illicit wares 75

"It's going to stall!" gasped the girl. "I *know* it's going to stall!" 101

"If you get out safely, there's no reason for me to ruin *my* clothes!" 171

"Look!" said Hazzard, pointing shakily. "L— look —— look ——!" 223

"I am sorry if you don't like Harry. . . ." . . 233

The nublick rose, and descended, smashing down the hinder edge of the bowl-like cavity, and tearing the ball free 299

The ball never deviated from the line; it ran pleasantly to the zinc, and tinkled home . . 329

ALIBI

IN the grill-room at Warwick every stranger and every guest is presumed innocent and truthful to the last degree of stern integrity; it is only when he steps out upon the turf, accepts a card from the caddy master, and takes his first practice swing near the first tee that he becomes an object of humorous interest and grave suspicion. No fairway was ever seriously injured by clubhouse conversation, and to this extent, therefore, any alien's claim to a seasonal average of eighty-five is undisputed; but statistics show that the man who in the grill-room prophesies eighty-five or better for his initial round at Warwick generally manages to turn in a score of about a hundred and ten; and this sweeping statement includes both the type of golfer who can excavate more rapidly with a spoon than a longshoreman with a shovel; and also the seasoned veteran who, like a field marshal in retreat, proceeds from one strategic position to another, chosen carefully in advance. They may know golf, but they don't know Warwick; and as they lag wearily to the players' entrance, after completing the round, they

3

are mentally competent to appreciate the fugitive verse painted in small letters above the door. The underlying thought is one which a circuit judge is said to have conceived with respect to a certain Miss Muller. It is n't humorous. [*]

Seen from the elevation of the veranda, the course is beautiful rather than suggestive of good golf; it presents the cultivated appearance of a millionaire's lawn, landscaped by the king of expert gardeners. Trees by Corot and brooks by Inness lie in a background of charming composition; vast reaches of lawn in the middle distance temper the glare of sunlight; far to the east a Maxfield Parrish harbor sleeps peacefully beneath a blanket of clouds by Elmer Ellsworth Garnsey. The sheer sweep of turf is nowhere marred by unsightly sand-pits; the ungainly cop-bunker is visible not at all. Save for the occasional oasis of a putting-green, and an occasional direction-flag whipping in the breeze, the links might pass for a deer-park or a national reservation. Obviously, to the stranger on the veranda, it is too well manicured to offer the highest phase of sport. It is too refined. It lacks the complications without which no true golfer can be content. It should be maintained exclusively in behalf of poets and artists; surely it is n't a test course for a red-blooded human being equipped

[*] Reference to John Greenleaf Whittier's "Maud Muller"

"For of all sad words of tongue or pen,
The saddest are these, 'It might have been.'"

with a leaden-weighted driver and a heavy mashie which scars the ground at every shot. Why, for a man to take turf at Warwick would be equivalent to mayhem!

But the professional who supervised the engineering was by birth a seer, and a bushwhacker by self-culture. To estimate from the craftiness displayed in his handiwork, he could unquestionably have ambushed an Apache in broad daylight in the middle of a field as level and unobstructed as a billiard-table. Not merely against par does one compete at Warwick; certainly not against the decrepit and long-since outlawed Colonel Bogey; not even primarily against an opponent in the flesh: the game is really played from start to finish against the fiendish imagination and Scottish ingenuity of Donald Ross. Witness the unexpected, hanging, side-hill lies; witness the undulating greens of almost impossible keenness; witness the apparent paucity of hazards, and the seeming infrequency of rough, and the astonishing presence of one or the other obstacle whenever a shot strays slightly from the line of geometrical progress. The dainty brook by Inness, the trees by Corot, so stand that to avoid them the study of triangulation is utterly essential. That soft bandeau of taller grass, posing calmly as the most inconsequential species of difficulty, proves to be the falsest of beards concealing behind it the identity of swamp and swale. An impenetrable morass masquerades, from the clubhouse, as a landscape garden. Hardly an artificial bunker or trap impedes the player in his journey from tee to green; everywhere his gaze falls upon the natural coloring of a well-kept lawn, but in some places the blades rise three inches higher than they do in other places. So that the amateur record is still pegged firmly at seventy-two.

On a certain particularly attractive morning in July, Mr. Robert Nixon, President, and Mr. Samuel Bowker, Chairman of the Finance Committee, of the Warwick Country Club, met by appointment in the New York office of a vast and soulless corporation dealing in real estate. Five minutes later they were staring in horror-stricken amazement at the diffident gentleman who temporarily controlled their golfing destinies. He was a gentleman of original and pregnant ideas; they could easily discern this fact from the frown which he wore as a part of his business garb, and from the aggressive forward thrust of his shoulders, which brought his chest into moderately justified prominence.

"Unfortunately — for you," said Mr. Fogarty, again breaking the silence, "our purpose in conducting this company — our ulterior motive, if I may say so — is to sell real property. The Warwick Realty Company is n't an eleemosynary institution in any sense of the word. Already we 've renewed the lease of your golf club two years beyond the limit we originally set; we can't renew it further. Of course, if you 're prepared to *buy* —"

"What I can't understand," protested Nixon vehemently, "is what prevented you from giving us a little notice. We expected *that* courtesy from you, at least!"

Mr. Fogarty spread his hands, intentionally expressive.

"As I said before, it was pure oversight on the part of the accounting department, but you knew the conditions. And, anyway, our business is n't to publish notices; it 's to sell real property —"

"What 's your price?" demanded Bowker, compressing his jaws. He was an earnest citizen, and his manner was invariably funereal; now and then it gave an indication of eagerness, as in the present instance.

"The price is five hundred thousand dollars."

"What!" Nixon motioned, incredulous. "You 're joking!"

"The exact amount," said Mr. Fogarty, complacently, "that we should expect to receive, gross, if we developed that property and sold it at the current acreage figures."

"And you won't take into consideration the desirability — and the importance to *you* — of having the club in Warwick? You've still got seven or eight hundred acres, Mr. Fogarty. Won't the very existence of the golf club help you sell them? Isn't it one of your biggest assets? Isn't it worth *something* to your company to keep the club alive?"

"Not a nickel," denied Mr. Fogarty, flatly. "Land is land. The only price I can quote you is the one I quoted, and the very best I can do is to sell you an option until the first of September. I'll do that for a thousand dollars."

"How about mortgages?" asked Nixon.

"One mortgage of two hundred thousand for three years, the balance in cash."

Mr. Bowker gasped, and clamped his jaws more tightly yet.

"But, look here! you must know the status of the club tract! In the open market it isn't worth more than sixty or seventy per cent. of what you're asking for it! We couldn't get a second mortgage of any size; you're making us put up pretty nearly three hundred thousand dollars *cash!*"

"Precisely," agreed Mr. Fogarty, without emotion. " That is, if you want to keep on playing that fool game. Otherwise — not ! "

Bowker reflected upon the terms, and shook his head, forgetting for some time to stop.

" It 's out of the question," he stated finally. " The club is n't a bank, Mr. Fogarty. We 've comparatively few wealthy members; we have n't encouraged them to join. We want men who play *golf*. And it 's been something of a strain to pay the overhead as it is. Even so, I think we might come to some mutually satisfactory agreement on the basis of an increased rental —"

" No," said Mr. Fogarty, yawning thoroughly; " we 're selling the property. It 's immaterial to us whether you or some one else takes it off our hands; but we 're selling it. We want to make one deal, and clean it up. If you fellows want a little leeway; if you think you 'll gain anything by putting it up to your members, I 'll arrange for a formal option. It 'll cost you just a thousand. If you don't take it up we 'll have to make plans to begin development work in the near future. The *very* near future. Just one thing more: Please don't come to us with counter-propositions, because we can't entertain them. We 'll take a three-year, first mortgage at two hundred thousand, and three hundred thousand cash. If you like, we 'll try to place a second mortgage for you on commission, but we won't carry it ourselves. That, I think, covers it."

Nixon drew a long, long breath.

"It seems so."

Mr. Fogarty was pained at his bruskness.

"My dear Mr. Nixon, you misunderstand me completely. This is nothing but a straightforward business arrangement to sell land which we own; you're taking it as a personal matter. I'm sorry. But the point now is; do you want an option?"

"Have it drawn!" said Bowker, morosely.

"Very well. Send me your check, and I'll mail it to you?"

"We'd better take it with us," said Bowker. "We'd better show it to the governing board. If we told 'em your price, and did n't have the evidence with us, they'd think we were fooling."

"Just as you like," conceded Mr. Fogarty, smiling blandly. "If you'll wait perhaps ten minutes —" He rang for his stenographer; Nixon looked at Bowker, Bowker glared at Nixon. Simultaneously, they read each other's thoughts.

"I *was* going out to play," confessed the president in an undertone. "Wonder if we ought to go down town and see the banks?"

"Wait until it rains," advised Bowker. "Too

good a day to waste time on bankers. Are you made up for the afternoon yet?"

"Not yet."

"We need a man. Want to come in?"

"Gladly. What are you doing?"

"Oh, around eighty-five."

"Really?" Nixon's astonishment was in the nature of flattery.

"Fairly regularly."

"Well, I have n't had a club in my hands for two weeks, but I 'll do about ninety myself."

"Bet you the caddy hire you don't."

"No-o," declined the president, cautiously; "I have n't touched a club for so long. But I 'll tell you what I *will* do; I 'll bet the caddy hire you are n't under a hundred."

"No-o," said Bowker. "You see, I just bought a new midiron; I 'm likely to be a bit off this afternoon. Oh, are you ready for us?"

"Sign here, please," said Mr. Fogarty, cheerfully.

By the first of August the Warwick Country Club was gloomily contemplating the prospect of immediate dissolution. Committees and subcommittees had been appointed and disbanded with all that celerity which obtains in Balkan ministries;

money had been subscribed, and pledges taken, and promises made, and yet the total amount involved was n't a quarter of the amount required. Bowker had toured the banks, and returned in discomfiture.

"They all admit," he said savagely, "that in a few years the land *will* be worth that much, but they can't see it *now*. They won't gamble with us. I 'm through, fellows. I 've done everything *I* can! It 's no use. The best thing for us to do is to get our names up for some other club as soon as we can."

"I 'm afraid so," granted Horton, the club champion. "There really was n't much use trying; you can't raise three hundred thousand among three hundred members in a little club of *this* kind."

"When you 're all through talking," said Nixon, "I 'll tell you something I 've been holding back. I know one man — a person — who *might* finance the whole thing for us; he has the money."

"Don't wake me up," said Bowker, softly.

"Perfectly true," insisted Nixon. "And the reason I 've been holding back is because I don't know what to do."

"It ought to be easy," said Horton. "Simply go in and ask him for a loan of three hundred thousand dollars for a few years. What 's simpler than that?"

"Sarcasm aside," reprimanded the president, "nothing *could* be simpler than that!"

"Do you mean to say you know a possible way out of this mess, and you have n't even begun to negotiate?"

"That's exactly what I do mean. The man happens to be a sort of relative of my wife. He's got three or four million, I suppose — retired a few years ago. He was in steel. Incidentally, he's buying nothing but suburban real estate just now."

Bowker sat up.

"Well, what *have* you been doing?"

"Thinking," said Nixon. "I don't doubt for a minute that if I could get my man out here, let him look over the land, investigate values, and all that, he'd consider helping us out — at a fat profit to himself, of course. Naturally I can't guarantee what he *would* do, but I think he'd be willing to give us some cash or take a· big bond and mortgage. Perhaps he'd even buy the property outright and let us have a long lease. It's only a chance, but —"

"Then why have n't you done something about it? Why have n't you sounded him?"

Nixon grinned in deprecation.

"He plays golf."

"Well, is n't that all the *better?*"

"Hardly. Let me explain. Cuyler — that's the man's name — Cuyler's sixty-seven years old. He took up the game ten years ago. Up to that time he could n't even talk about it intelligently; to-day his improvement is inconceivable."

"Plays pretty well, does he?"

"No," said Nixon; "*talks.* Honestly, he could give Jerry Travers two adjectives a hole, and beat him without more than half trying. You listen to him before he goes out or after he comes back, and you 'll think he broke the world's record. But in the meantime —"

"Yes?"

"I 've played this game for a good many years," said Nixon, "and I 've seen some wonderful exhibitions. I 've seen men lose their tempers, and I 've seen them break their clubs. I 've seen them throw whole bags of clubs into the pond. I 've heard some alibis that would have given Ananias material for another couple of centuries. But when old John Cuyler gets up to the tee — well, it 's a new chapter."

"*Still*, I don't see your argument."

"If I brought him out here," explained Nixon, patiently, "he 'd have to be entertained. He 's been a big man, an influential man; he 's always had attention, and he loves it. There 'd have to be a luncheon before the game — incidentally, he never plays in the morning. If he were n't entertained he 'd never forget it; so it would n't do to prejudice him unfavorably before the start. All right. During luncheon he 'd begin to talk. He 'd talk some of the best golf you ever heard in your life; and he 's so constituted that he sees the events of last month through a lovely golden haze of romance. If he made a certain hole in seven, he 'll figure afterwards that if he 'd putted another inch to the right, he 'd have been down in six. Morally he 's sure it *was* six — a constructive six, that is. Fine! Then a little later he 'll remember that his drive was a few yards in the rough, and it cost him a stroke to get out. If his drive had been straight, he 'd have saved a stroke. Good! He knows he could have made a five instead of a six if he 'd tried a tiny bit harder, and kept out of trouble. Morally at least a five, then. But if his approach had gone ten yards farther — you ought to get the idea by this time. I 've played Montclair with him when he made a hundred and twenty-one; two weeks afterward it was ninety-nine; about now he 'll claim he did Montclair in eighty-seven, and he 'll describe every stroke in detail! "

" He 's on the road to be a regular player," said Bowker.

"To continue. He recites these things and then goes out, and for three or four holes he'll put in a string of excuses and defenses that'll stagger you. Then when he sees that it won't do — he'll go sky-high! What he'll say or what he'll do is beyond my wildest fancy. Besides, he rarely repeats; it's new stuff every time. I'll tell you this much: he invests in a good many schemes, he plays a good deal of golf, but there isn't a case on record when he was *sold* on the links. It can't be done. He keeps his mind on the game. Furthermore, he's never yet done business with a man he played with beforehand. He's too much chagrined and morti-fied and full of conscience. And certainly he wouldn't consider buying this golf property without playing here. If he does, and if he plays his best game, he won't better a hundred and twenty, be-cause this is the stiffest course in the district. Dur-ing the round he'll say some things that'll stop business right there. And we're the people who'll have to play with him; we can't get out of it. If we do take him around, we're lost before we start. I *know.* Why, we were playing Montclair with a man who thought he was persuading Cuyler to come in with him on a scheme which would, and eventu-ally *did,* net two hundred per cent. Before we got off, Cuyler talked in the low eighties. He was

twenty-nine for four holes. On the fifth he accused the other man of sneezing so as to spoil a
putt, and it was all over. Now, that's the only
chance *I* have! Remember, we're not asking for
a loan of personality; we want cash, or credit. If
you want to risk your peace of mind, I'll risk mine,
and we'll have him out here —"

"If he happened to have some luck," said Horton, slowly, "it wouldn't hurt us, would it?"

"We might use the ladies' tees," added Bowker.
"That would cut ten strokes off his score, anyway."

"What's the best he's ever done?"

"Why, a hundred and four or five," said Nixon.
"At Gedney Farm."

"That's equivalent to a hundred and twenty
here," said Horton, reflectively.

"Only about a hundred and ten from the short
tees, though," persisted Bowker. "Would that
satisfy him, do you think?"

Nixon, who had been drumming on the table with
his fountain-pen, suddenly ceased.

"Wait a second!"

"Got a mortal thought, Bobby?"

"Possibly. I wonder —"

"Don't disturb him!" said Horton.

Nixon brought his hand in startling contact with
the champion's knee.

"*I've* got it!"

Horton grimaced.

"I realize *that,* old top; but you did n't need to flatten it out entirely!"

"No, listen! All we need is a thousand dollars and three weeks' time —"

"I 'll contribute the time," promised Bowker, "if you 'll advance the money. What 's the idea?"

The president beamed upon them beatifically.

"Both of you be here at nine o'clock Monday morning without fail! Can you do that? And by the way, how much confidence do you think the club has in me?"

"All there is. Why?"

"Because on Sunday night," stated Nixon, "the club-house and the links are going to close up tighter than a drum for three weeks! By virtue of the authority vested in me — for the good of the people and all that sort of thing! The club-house and the whole course will close for three solid weeks, and I don't intend to give anybody any reasons! That is, except to you two. Will you come?"

"Why — yes," they agreed, bewildered.

From the moment that they sat down to lunch with Mr. Cuyler, both Horton and Bowker recognized the truth of the president's description of

him.   He was a short, stout man, dominantly forceful and incisive and bristling with conscious energy;
his manner invited, and yet defied contradiction.
Having seated himself and unfurled his napkin with
snap and vigor, he opened fire point-blank; without
delaying for a preliminary skirmish.

"A pretty course — a pretty course from up
here," he began. "Looks so easy, though; not
enough trouble. Par seventy-two? That's fair
enough. Suppose you young fellows crack eighty
right along. I'm not in *your* class; *I*'m satisfied
with eighty-five or so. Bob, did you hear I've got
to cut it out?"

"Not cut out *golf?*" inquired Nixon.

"Yes, sir; so I'm told. Say, it's hurting me.
I can't see it, but I look at it this way: what do
they *gain* by telling me quit? Answer, nothing at
all. Can't be mercenary, can it? Next reason,
I'm not fool enough to pay a specialist — best specialist in the world — a couple of thousand a year
for advice, and then not take it. So pretty soon I'll
have to stop. Not yet, though. I've got a year
or two left in me."

Bowker kicked Horton under the table.

"Er — you 'll be glad to have played Warwick,"
said Horton, desperately.

"I daresay, sir. Heard a lot about it; very

hard, they tell me. Long carries." He nodded rapidly, and put his fist on the table, as though in preparedness for disputation.

"Nixon tells us you're a long driver, though," remarked Bowker.

"Very long at times, very long indeed. Out at Montclair I was driving *very* well — remember it, Bob?"

"You surely were," said Nixon.

"What was it I made that day? Eighty-nine, I think. Somewhere around there. It was a bad day, extremely bad. It's an easy course; any lady ought to get around under ninety. I'm likely to play very well or very badly, gentlemen. Don't be alarmed, whatever happens. If I'm on my game, I may give you a rub. I startle the youngsters once in a while — eh, Bob?"

"A great many good players do poorly the first time around Warwick," said Nixon, gravely. "There's no doubt that it's the hardest course in the East, anyway."

"Let's be at it?" said Cuyler, impatiently. "Hurry up with that lunch!"

As the quartet emerged from the clubhouse, half an hour later, the capitalist paused, and surveyed the panorama which spread lazily out before him in the sunshine.

" Nice view you've got," he said. " How much belongs to you? "

" Over two hundred acres," Nixon told him. " The land across the road is held at five thousand an acre, but of course that's well developed."

Mr. Cuyler assented by means of a spasmodic jerk of the head.

" Looks like a good buy. We'll talk business later, Bob. It's better than I expected. Wouldn't mind having it in my own family. Well, where do we begin? "

" The first hole," said Horton, " is just over the brow of the first hill. You have a card, haven't you? "

Mr. Cuyler, by a sudden gesture, conveyed the idea that he had a bushel of them.

" Thanks. Three hundred and ninety yards. How far does that rough go? "

" A hundred and eighty. It isn't the sort of rough you're probably used to; it's simply good grass about four inches high," cautioned Horton.

" Shoot! " said Mr. Cuyler. " Show me the way, somebody! "

The champion drove prettily; Nixon and Bowker followed; the capitalist stood on the tee and waved his driver threateningly.

" I haven't had a club in my hands for nineteen

days," he explained, "and my hands are cold. Never mind; I'll scratch along somehow." He drove stiffly, cleared the taller grass, and was delighted to perceive his ball within twenty yards of Horton's.

"Beautiful drive, Mr. Cuyler," said Bowker in his ear. "Horton's champion of the club,— handicapped five in the metropolitan,— and he hit his ball perfectly, too."

"Oh, I get 'em off now and then. That was half-topped. Brassey, boy!" He sclaffed it badly, but the ball rolled to the summit of the little hill, and dipped toward the hollow.

"You're on!" called Horton. "Good shot!"

They all made fours; as they proceeded to the second tee, Mr. Cuyler was moved to eloquence.

"Any man who takes more than four on that hole," he proclaimed, "ought to be put off the course. Three hundred and ninety yards is a short hole. I could have made it with a drive and a mashie. I could have had a try for a birdie. Can't expect to use the right clubs when I don't know where the flag is." He imbedded his ball in an immense cone of sand. "Don't suppose any of you brought a pair of gloves? Well, never mind; only it ends *me*. Can't hold on to a club without 'em; it turns right over in my hand." He lunged powerfully, and surveyed the result for several tense seconds. " Well, that 's a shot any baby 'd be proud of! I was figuring on the wind taking it, and —"

" Baby!" echoed Bowker. " Man alive, you 're half-way to the green!"

" No!" Nevertheless, Mr. Cuyler stood on tip toe, and craned his neck perilously.

" Look at it! It did n't carry far, but it must have rolled a hundred and fifty yards."

" I don't know what it is," said Mr. Cuyler, speaking gently, in order that Nixon would not overhear him, " but usually I get an enormous roll on the ball. Have n't the least idea what does it. Something I do to it, I suppose."

" You keep on hitting 'em the same way," said Horton, sagely, " and you 'll make a good score."

" It 's a fearful handicap; I don't know the distances," said Mr. Cuyler. " Don't know the lay of the land, either. It makes half a dozen strokes difference, too. Play to left or right of the green?"

" The left, by all means, and well to the left," counseled Horton, withdrawing out of his scope of vision.

Mr. Cuyler sliced thirty degrees to the right.

" I knew it," he said bitterly. " The confounded caddy stood right where I could see him out of the tail of my eye. He moved, too. Boy, think you 're on exhibition? Did you mark that ball? Know where it is?" He went forward, elucidating the caddy's pedigree to him as he went. The others played up to the green; Mr. Cuyler found himself hole high, in grass to his shoe-tops. "If I only had a mashie-niblick," he accused the caddy. "This deep-faced toothpick is n't balanced right. Still —" He chipped out to the green, and took two putts; and overcome by the realization that his score was good, he regarded the ball pridefully and stole furtive glances at his partners. Once he made as though to speak to Nixon, but chose the part of discretion, and resumed his endeavor to appear diffident.

"Did you see him play his third?" said Horton to Bowker, very loudly. "He talks about playing in the eighties. I don't believe he ever made an eighty in his life; he makes seventies." The capitalist, who had started angrily, became calmer at the conclusion of the last sentence.

"I should have been on in two," he asserted, still holding Nixon with his eye. "Absolutely threw away a stroke. My regular game, though — throw away one stroke every hole. Well, I got a five; should have been a four. I was saying, if I had a mashie-niblick I 'd have *had* a four. Well, I 'm one over four for two holes. Where's the next one?"

They showed it to him. On the right, parallel with the line, ran a row of trees cunningly planted in echelon; on the left, a boundary wall of jagged stones. Curling delicately around the green, a brook offered lodging to any transient ball which left the straightest route or overran. Between this and the tee lay luxuriant grass which was evidently retentive of what came within its reach.

"Not having had a club in my hands for nineteen days," said Mr. Cuyler, "I *may* not make it. I see you've got to land on the green, and stick. And there's a blister coming right where I hold the club. I may not do it; probably I won't. He didn't; but the ball bobbed and bounced downhill until at last it trickled within a dozen feet of the hole and came to rest. Mr. Cuyler looked at the gash he had cut in the tee; he examined critically the head of his driver. "Little muscular strain in my shoulder," he admitted. "Had a touch of neuritis last night. It's a wonder I can get 'em off the ground."

"If there hadn't been power behind it," said Bowker, "you wouldn't have. That's what got you through." He pitched squarely on the flag; the ball bounced nimbly into the brook.

25

" You hesitate at the top of your swing," opined Mr. Cuyler, helpfully. " You'll pardon me for saying so, but it's very noticeable." He marched dignifiedly down to his ball, and took three skittish putts. " One over four for *three* holes," he stated, fighting down his pride. " And if the architecture of your course is anywhere nearly logical, the next hole ought to be a long one."

" Five hundred and thirty yards," said Nixon. " You want to clear the brook on your drive, that's all."

" Don't you think he'd better play safe?." objected Bowker. " It's a fearful carry — have him go short."

Mr. Cuyler, sniffing with contempt addressed his ball gingerly. Success had startled and shocked him; and upset his none too stable poise. His hands were inconveniently trembling, and his shoulders sagged limply; but his mouth was firmly set; and his eyes showed indomitable resolution, mixed with unholy fear.

" If you gentlemen will stop talking," he mumbled. " It throws me off; it always *throws* me off." In his anxiety he touched the ball, so that it toppled from its nest of sand. " There!" he snapped. " That's what I get for it! Took my mind off it! Enough to rattle *any*body. It makes you stiffen up

— and —" Here he drove with admirable precision into the second brook. There was a silver splash in the sunshine, a dot of white on the fairway ahead.

" *Out*, by George!" breathed Bowker.

" You hit that hard," said Horton, appreciatively. " *How* you do get your hips into it!"

" Right on your drive to-day," said Nixon.

The capitalist faced them frowningly.

" I don't know what it is," he admitted; " it's beyond *me!* No matter how I hit 'em, they *go!* I must put something on the ball." He clipped the heads from a pair of misplaced daisies. " It was the follow-through that saved me," he reported. " The shot was rotten — all but the follow-through. That saved it. That always comes when I need it. And it's funny, because I don't feel like playing golf to-day. I don't believe I slept three hours last night." With his hand shading his eyes, he watched the flight of Horton's ball, a straight, clean drive which escaped the water hazard by the barest of margins. " How far do you estimate that shot?" he demanded.

" He averaged two hundred and thirty off the tee in the championship," said Nixon. " I guess that's further, though."

" My reason for asking," said Mr. Cuyler, smiling a trifle cynically as Bowker pulled into trouble, " is that I wondered how far mine went. I think I could do better if my shoulders were n't tied up into bow-knots with neuritis." He topped his second savagely, and analyzed the effort with a wealth of imagery. His third attempt was successful enough to justify a putter on the fourth. " Down in five," he bragged, glowing rapturously and breathing hard.

" Five," said Horton.

" Six," said Nixon.

" Six," said Bowker.

" I am almost sorry," proclaimed the capitalist, drying the moisture from his clammy hands, " that I 'm starting so well. Of course it 's nothing extraordinary, but I seem to be one over par for four holes. It 's too good; it distresses me. Ought not to keep medal scores at all — that 's my theory. They distract you. Now I 'll probably press; natural for anybody. I wish I had n't lost a stroke on the second; I 'd be even with par."

" You 're steady as a church," said Nixon. " Keep it up."

" You 've made only one mistake in four holes," said Bowker.

" I thought I was a long driver," said Horton

28

aggrievedly, " but you 're right with me every shot — except when you 're ahead of me."

Mr. Cuyler stared at the lofty hill which confronted him.

" There 's one thing about it," he proclaimed through chattering teeth. " I — I 've got nerve enough, but against this wind, with a heavy ball — — well, it 's all in the day's work. What 's the odds? We 're out for fun, are n't we ? "

" You bet we are," Bowker assured him heartily. " We all play for the fun of it."

Here Mr. Cuyler hooked viciously; almost before the club-head had passed the ball he was scrutinizing it with every symptom of apoplexy.

" Oh, the idiots!" he rasped. " The miserable, lying, cheating, swindling idiots! Look! Look at that! Feel of that club! It 's new; just had it made. Took it out of the bag to-day for the first time. Feel where the balance is! You feel of that! *Heft* it! There 's *two ounces* too much lead back there! Feel it turn over of its own weight at the top of the swing! The idea of trying to play golf with a stuffed mallet like that! Now I 'm mad! I 'll tell you exactly what 'll happen: I 'll dub every shot from here to the finish. Watch me ! "

Accordingly, they watched him dub two of them, and run down an approach putt for a par four.

"That's the principle of it," praised Bowker. "Go right after 'em!"

"Great recovery, Mr. Cuyler!" said Horton. "That's the sort of play what wins matches!"

"You can't beat him," declared Nixon. "When he's in the mood for it."

But the capitalist was shaking from head to foot. Despite his theory, he had requisitioned a card from his caddy, and recorded his own score; twice, as he was making the entries, the pasteboard fluttered from his palsied fingers.

"Four," he whispered. "One over four, one over four, two over four, two over four. I'm two over four for five holes!" Here he dropped the pencil.

"Your shot, Mr. Cuyler."

"Where?" he inquired weakly. They indicated a yellow flag which, to his disordered fancy, marked a hill at least a mile and a half to westward. "My wrists have gone back one me," he muttered. "Broke one of 'em a few years ago. They've gone back; afraid to *hit* a ball any more. And if I try to spare it, I'll fluff it. Hardest shot for anybody in the world's a spared shot. Besides . . . my s-h-o-e p-i-n-c-h-e-s. . . . The mere momentum of the club carried the ball out in soaring flight; Mr. Cuyler sat down hard on the tee-box and mopped his glistening countenance. His expression, as he looked at Corbett, was the harbinger of speech, but he thought better of it, and kept silence, although the repression must have tortured him.

"Bully?" said Bowker. "You'll be under forty for nine holes!"

Mr. Cuyler reacted as though he had received a gratuitous insult.

"Oh, no, I won't! You don't know me! You're a *young* man. *I* can't climb around these hills; all out of breath when I come to my second shot. I'll miss it *sure.*"

He dubbed it indeed, but it rolled leisurely to the green, and stayed there. He putted, and the ball sank with a gratifying tinkle.

"Three for me," he said, fumbling for the card and again dropping his pencil, which the caddy retrieved. "Three, and it's a par four! It's three hundred and sixty yards; it's uphill — a birdie three! I'm one over four for six holes." He stretched his arms wide, and inhaled deeply. "Gad! what a wonderful course!" he said. "A *wonderful* course! It's the hardest in the metropolitan district,— everybody says so,— and I'm one over four for six holes! Didn't expect me to be going so strong, did you? Where's the next? Where's the seventh?"

"Foot of the hill," Bowker told him. "It's long, but it's very easy. All you have to do is to swipe it clean; she'll roll indefinitely."

Obediently, Mr. Cuyler swiped it. He caught the ball on the toe of the club; it glanced to the right, found the slope, and leaped amazingly downward. Mr. Cuyler, posing rigidly in the attitude in which all experts are photographed, tarried until his muscles ached.

"Foundered," he said, "but it rolled! *Did n't* it roll! I don't know what it is, but I put some stuff on 'em. It must be something I do to it; *I* don't know! But they certainly do roll for me."

The other three all outdrove him, but his soul was immune to envy. He found his ball in a hanging lie: but his exaltation rose superior to his woe. Wild-eyed and panting, he swung badly; but it was beyond his power to nullify the influence of a twenty per cent. grade, and he had a short putt for a three. The ball hung on the lip of the cup; Mr. Cuyler whirled toward his caddy.

"There you go again!" he roared. "You coughed! You do that once more —"

"*In!*" cried Bowker behind him.

"What? Did it go down?"

"It fiddled around and then dropped. Look in the cup!"

"A three for Mr. Cuyler," said Horton, noting it.

"Even fours to here," commented Nixon. "That's remarkable, especially for a man who never saw the place before to-day."

"But I'm so sore at that idiot of a caddy," growled Mr. Cuyler, "I'm likely to go all to pieces any minute. The idea! Coughing when a man's going to putt! Just my luck, anyway. I *always* draw boys like that! . . . Wish I'd had some gloves with me. Well, now for a short slice and a merry one! Take me ten strokes for this one, I suppose; lucky if I get around under fifty."

As a matter of fact, he finished the first nine holes in an even forty, smashing his best previous record on any course by thirteen strokes, and when they led him to the clubhouse, he took stimulants more from necessity than from inclination.

It was an hour before they could persuade him back to the links.

"I'm satisfied," he told them again and again. "You gentlemen go ahead. I'm tired. Nine holes is plenty for an old man, anyhow."

"Not by the wildest stretch of the imagination," corrected Horton, gallantly, "can a man be called old when he can go out in forty at Warwick!"

Eventually, however, they cajoled him out, and once more he paused to survey and to admire the landscape.

"What rent do you boys pay for this?" he asked.

"Twenty thousand," said Nixon.

"I should want thirty; that's six per cent. on the investment. Where's the next hole?"

Joyously they chorused directions for reaching the tenth, which was guarded by another of the Inness brooks and by a semicircle of trees.

"Almost wish I hadn't said I'd play," the man of money complained to them. "Sat too long in the house; got cold." Thus armed with a reasonable excuse, he drove almost at right angles to the course.

"Too bad!" said Horton, sorrowfully. "I'm afraid you're in a rough spot."

"You're right it's too bad," murmured Nixon.

"Just cold — nothing but cold," explained Mr. Cuyler. "Serves me right; ought to have had more sense. Now I can't relax in the swing." He took four shots in the rough, gouged four tremendous clots of sod, approached execrably, putted miserably, and was down in nine. His subsequent monologue was illuminating; his powers of improvisation excelled even Nixon's promises. The three conspirators stole covert glances at one another as they walked to the eleventh tee.

" We think we 're extravagant if we play for a ball a hole," whispered Nixon to Bowker. " But you won't think it 's so funny if it turns out that we played the tenth to-day for half a million — and lost ! "

" Give him a chance ! " said Bowker, mirthlessly.

The eleventh was rated on the card as a par five; Mr. Cuyler, assisted by a flat stone at the root of a tree, accomplished it in seven, splintered his putter over his knee, and kicked his tweed hat into the brook. Having filed this mute objection to the mandates of the gods, he palpitated, and wiped his eyes.

" Now I 've strained my thumb ! " he said pathetically. " Never mind; come ahead ! Everything breaks against me. I don't care; I play for the fun of it. It keeps me out in the open air. There 's the deuce of a wind, too. If that caddy eats another apple with as much noise as he did the last one I 'll brain him. That 's a fair warning. *Take it !* "

The twelfth was a simple iron shot; he played it professionally, got his three, and smiled in manifest dejection.

35

"Nineteen for three holes," he observed. "Great golf! One over six! Could n't be worse if I 'd only used one hand. It amounts to that anyway — with this shoulder. And now I 've got to putt with a cleek!"

"Lend you my putter," said three voices in unison. He shook his head.

"Oh, no. No use, anyway. I 'm done. My nerves are all shot to pieces. First time in my life I ever had a drink between rounds. No chance now. Is this a long one?"

"It 's a dog-leg. Straight out," said Horton, and a moment later he added: "That 's absolutely perfect. Fifteen feet off that line, and you 'd have been either out of bounds or in the rough."

Mr. Cuyler stood aghast at the compliment.

"But — but that was a hook!"

"Exactly. And as prettily placed a hook as I ever saw in my life."

"Darned clever," said Bowker. "I wish *I* knew how to play for a hook."

"Oh, he 's an old fox," said Nixon. "I told you so."

"It . . . it *was* pretty fair," conceded Mr. Cuyler, modestly, "but if I 've got to play many more of these blind holes I 'll be so muddled I can't hit a balloon. I 'll be hooking instinctively." Nevertheless, he brought off another shot which Horton promptly characterized as superlative; and in reality it was thirty yards from the pin. An approach and two putts gave him his five.

The fourteenth tee was on the edge of a sickening swamp, inhabited by bullfrogs which croaked malevolently. Once more a battery of trees was placed to penalize a slice; on the left an artistic rockery glinted in the sun.

"If those darned frogs would only shut up," said Mr. Cuyler, warmly, "perhaps I could give some attention to this ball. How far is it across the Gulf of Mexico?"

"It's a good, full shot," they said, soberly.

"And a good, full shot is something a man of seventy — I'm nearly seventy — could n't make to save his life. Well, here goes. If I miss it, somebody'll have to loan me a dredge!" He drove neatly across the swamp; the ball rolled easily to the green. One after the other, Nixon, Bowker, and Horton topped among the frogs.

"Twenty-seven for five holes," said Mr. Cuyler, tremulously, "and I beat all three of you! Are there any more Everglades, or do you play the rest of the way on dry land? Say, I'm shivering! This place is n't malarial, is it?"

"We go right back across it," said Nixon; "but

this time it's shorter. Don't take any chances. Use a high tee, and slam it."

Mr. Cuyler annihilated him with a single glance.

"If there's anything that puts me off my game quicker than anything else," he lectured, "it's to have a man advise me. I wish you had n't said that. From my friends I want friendship only; when I need advice, I go to an expert." While the trio stood motionless, agonized, he drove a dead, high ball, which missed the water by an eyelash, and permitted him to make his five in spite of a poor second shot. "You pretty nearly made me spoil that hole," he said severely. "I beg of you, don't do it again."

Bowker and Nixon were riotously shaking hands when the capitalist, in the act of driving, turned quickly upon them.

"Blast it!" he said wrathfully. "What are you two trying to do? Do you *want* to throw me off my game? Can't anybody in this whole crowd stand still when I'm going to shoot?"

"I'm sorry," said Nixon, hastily.

"You ought to be!" He returned to the ball. "Blast it!" he repeated. "Something's wrong every hole. First it's a caddy, and then it is n't. You've got me shaking like a convict. Look at me!"

Indeed, his hands were strikingly unsteady.

"There's no hurry," soothed Horton. "Take your time, Mr. Cuyler."

"Oh, another counselor!" He breathed hard, and swung his club. "If I were n't a guest here —" Choking with anger, he slashed at the ball, and saw it disappear over a near-by ridge. "Is it safe?" he asked anxiously.

"Could n't be better!"

"You really should n't disturb a man who's driving, you know."

"We 're very sorry, Mr. Cuyler."

"I 'm going badly enough as it is without having to be rattled every minute."

"You 're doing excellently."

"I 'm glad you think so —"

"All you need is a three to be even fives for this round."

"Yes, but the way to have a man get three's is n't to saw at his nerves until they 're all on edge." In evident irritation he topped two brassey shots; the second was a yard from the green.

"Play it safe!" said Nixon, unthinking.

Mr. Cuyler, gritting his teeth, struck desperately with his mashie, and the ball ran unerringly to the cup and dropped. He looked at the cup, looked at

ALIBI

Nixon, opened his mouth, closed it again and said nothing.

"One over five!" said Horton, jubilantly. "You need two fours to break an eighty-five!"

The capitalist went through the motions of addressing, but his legs shook, and in the waggle he couldn't bring the face of his driver within six inches of the ball.

"How — far is it?" he faltered.

"Four hundred and twenty-five — a good four."

His face was ashen, and his mouth was working grotesquely as he swung. He heeled the ball; it wandered casually down a gentle slope, and found a cozy seat in a boot-mark.

"All over!" he said, gulping. "I'm all through. I'm cooked. Did the best I could; too much for me. I don't believe I can even lift the club."

"Try!" begged Horton. "You can make it up —"

"No, it's too late! I wasted a lot of strokes in the first nine; they'd have helped me here! It's too late now." He swung half-heartedly.

"Only one more!" urged Bowker at his elbow. "Just an ordinary iron. Get a five here and a three on the home hole, and you'll still have your eighty-four."

"No, I never have any luck." He could hardly hold the club the caddy gave him; he stared at it stupidly; when he finally employed it, the stroke was pecking, unorthodox, clumsy, and yet effective. It left him so close to the hole that he went down in two putts, one of a foot, the other of two inches; and he remained crouching until Nixon took him tenderly by the arm and escorted him to the last tee.

"Lots of nerve, Mr. Cuyler," he encouraged. "It's only a hundred and sixty yards. Just hit it cleanly; that's all you need. Don't bother about the brook or anything else. Just one more hole, *please!* You've done magnificently. I know you're tired, but you'll want to remember this. Take a few practice swings."

Bowker, who had been gesticulating violently as he talked to Horton, joined them, and stepped on Nixon's toe.

"They've changed the hole, Mr. Cuyler," he said. "They've shortened it. It's only about a hundred yards. Take a wooden club, and just tap it. You can't fall down now."

"Never mind about the practice swings; let him drive!" warned Horton. "Hurry up! *Speed!* Make him shoot, or he'll faint!"

Mr. Cuyler regarded his driver dispassionately.

" You know," he said almost inaudibly, " I 'm an old man — little touch of vertigo. If I 'd had my gloves with me — and my regular putter —"

There was a click of wood against gutta-percha; three men strained in unison. Horton emitted a yell of triumph, and without bothering to play his own ball, made for the green. Nixon and Bowker had the capitalist betwen them; they guided him carefully over the tiny foot-bridge, set him firmly in position, gave him a club — any club!

" Two putts, Mr. Cuyler! The regulation two! "

" Don't try to sink it; get near the hole."

" Play it right for here — where my hand is now. Easy! "

" Not too hard, whatever you do! It 's a fast green! "

" Don't hurry! Lots of time! "

" Get his club in line, Nixon! "

" It 's in line now."

" Don't let him hit it too hard! "

" No; just easy, Mr. Cuyler! Take two for it! "

" *Now* putt! "

Mr. Cuyler putted with a potent shove. The ball, traveling swiftly, struck the back of the tin, hopped nimbly upward, and was abruptly swallowed by the metallic haven of victory.

" Eighty-three! " gasped Horton, grasping his

hand. " You 're a wizard — you 're a wizard! " That made it unanimous; but Mr. Cuyler never heard the praise. He was swaying dreamily above the hole, and on his face the joy of all imaginings was shining peacefully.

It was eight o'clock before the guest of honor had recovered sufficiently to be assisted into the private dining-room; and it was ten o'clock before he was able to return thanks for the first toast.

" Boys," he said, " it was a fine day. I 'm glad it was, because it 's my last. I can't stand it. Getting too old, I guess. I 'm sorry, because if I had time to practise, I might be pretty good. But the time to quit is when you 're happy. It is n't a usual thing to drag business into pleasure, but I 'm going to this time. Bob Nixon here has been trying to get me interested in this club property. It looks good to me — as an investment, I mean. I understand you 've been in danger of losing your club. That won't happen. It 's a lovely club; it 's the best and the hardest course I ever played over. I made my best — I mean, I made a good score on it, and I had a couple of bad holes, too. Some of your holes are too short, but you 've got to play 'em with deadly accuracy. That 's how I made my score to-day — I was deadly accurate. Well, it 's too lovely a club to let go by default. So I'm going to take it over, and lease it to you for a term of years. All I ask from you, to please an old man's vanity, is your signatures on my card. You'll attest it for me, won't you?"

"Certainly we will," said Bowker, clearing his throat. "Is it — is it absolutely definite that you're through with golf?"

"Absolutely. I never change my mind after it's once made up. I'm done!"

Bowker rose, and went for the door.

"I'll be with you in a couple of minutes," he said. "I'm going to telephone the papers."

"Not about this purchase!" snapped Mr. Cuyler.

"No, sir; about your score. I think it's a matter of public interest — don't you, Bob?"

"No question about it," said Nixon stoutly. "It's a record all right — for a man nearly seventy."

The capitalist actually blushed.

"Well, in that case you might hint — only *hint*, of course — that — ah — I hadn't played Warwick before, and that — ah — unfortunately, I was suffering somewhat from rheumatism . . . you know. . . ."

"I'll have a paragraph on it," said Bowker, vanishing.

They took the financier to the station for the last train. After it had gone, the three sat on a baggage-truck and laughed themselves into incipient hysteria.

"Obtaining money under false pretenses," chuckled Horton, when he had recovered a fraction of his balance, "is nothing compared to this! And there 'll be murder if he ever finds it out."

"He can't. For *two* reasons; the other one is sentimental."

"That 's so," said Bowker, sobering. "You know, I really think he cried a little — from pure happiness. Poor old scout."

"It did n't harm anybody, did it? And it 's really a good investment, after all. Only —"

"When 'll the course be ready, Bob?"

"Day after to-morrow," said Nixon. "All we 've got to do is to cover up our tracks, put those temporary tees out of commission, change the flags back, change all the cups, and that sort of thing."

"If he ever comes out again —"

"Tell him we 've rebuilt the links and lengthened it. That 's simple."

"Has any one the least idea how long that course was?"

"I don't know how long it was," said Horton, "but with my own clubs I played it in sixty-one the day before yesterday, and fifty-nine yesterday. It must have been about four thousand yards for eighteen holes. A stranger would n't suspect the card; those hills and water hazards are too deceptive. The only thing *I* was afraid of was that he 'd spot the cups. Good Lord! they were as big as drainpipes! An extra inch in diameter! Why, those were n't cups; those were craters!"

"What got *me,*" snickered Bowker, "was the way you could take a free, healthy, natural swing at that ball with one of your patent drivers, and never get more than a hundred and forty yards with it! That was genius on your part — if we 'd used our regular wooden clubs he 'd have spotted us in a flash!"

"Why not?" asked Horton, surprisedly. "You could n't expect short-weight drivers to put distance into your shots, could you?"

"What was the weight?" asked Nixon, reminiscently.

"They averaged about eight ounces," said Horton. "That 's about what I ordered."

Perhaps it was best for Mr. Cuyler's repose of mind that after buying the property and leasing it to the club, he contracted gout and never visited Warwick again. Undoubtedly it was best for him that he had n't played his trial round on the regular course. Because if he had done that, he would n't have been consoled to the day of his death by the memory of his sterling 83, and he would certainly have been in no condition to appreciate the verse painted in small letters above the players' entrance to the clubhouse. As has been said before, it is n't humorous.

IF YOU DON'T MIND MY TELL-
ING YOU

MR. VALENTINE MOTT, scowling fero-
ciously, made a fierce gesture toward his
wife, five miles distant, and removed the hand
which he had fitted over the transmitter as soon as
the men in the nearest locker unit had begun to sing
" How Dry I Am! " in close and execrable harmony.   Mr. Mott leaned in utter impatience against
the wall, and glowered mercilessly at his distant
wife, and forthwith interrupted her in a voice
freighted with glucose and saccharin.

"Well, I'm awfully sorry," he said. "Yes, I
know I promised to come back for lunch; I know
all that. . . . I certainly did intend to come back,
but . . . Well, you know how it is; I met this
man, and he's a good customer of ours and he
wants me to play another round with him. I was
just getting ready to change my clothes when he
. . . Oh, I *could,* but I don't like to offend a man;
these big buyers are so touchy sometimes you
wouldn't hardly . . . Well, of *course;* but it's
the little personal attentions that count. It's a real

48

opportunity to get in solid with him. . . . Well, I
don't see exactly how I can get out of it now; he's
waiting for me at the first tee this minute. . . . I
hope you don't think I 'm *enjoying* it; it 's a cold-
blooded business proposition; we 're not really going out for the *golf;* he just sort of wants to walk
around for the exercise and talk business between
shots. . . . Well, I *would* bring him home, but he
wants the exercise. . . . Oh, absolutely! Why,
I 'll take you anywhere you say; I had n't planned
anything for to-morrow. . . . Not to-night, dear;
I can't go out anywhere to-night. . . . Yes, to-
morrow, and any night next week, too. . . . I certainly *don't!* . . . Well, I did n't even expect to
play this afternoon, and to-morrow I 'll drive you
anywhere you . . . Oh, it might easily mean a
thousand dollars to me. . . . Yes, a thousand. . . .
Just as soon as we finish. . . . Oh, no, I would n't
do that! The greens committee does n't like to
have women on the course on Saturdays. I 'll start
home the minute we finish. . . . All right; I 'm just
as sorry as you are. Good-by!"

Mr. Mott hung up the receiver, exhaled in an
abandon of relief, and smartly accosted a cadaverous friend, who happened to be passing through the
locker-room.

"Oh, Smithson! Made up yet for the afternoon?" Smithson paused, and shook his head disconsolately.

"I'm sorry, but I've got to go home, Val. Where's the crowd you had this morning?"

"They had to go home, too," said Mr. Mott, implying unutterable weakness on the part of the henpecked miscreants. "*I*'m going to play eighteen more."

"How in thunder do you do it?" asked the cadaverous one in frank envy and injured righteousness. "If I ever managed to get in thirty-six holes just *once* —"

Mr. Mott waved the hand which had recently done duty as a silencer.

"Easiest thing in the world. Mrs. Mott wouldn't any more think of spoiling my Saturdays than — well, she just wouldn't think of it. She knows I'm working like a dog all the week; a man's got to have *some* recreation."

"That's so; but I can't ever seem to get it over. Well, how were you shooting?"

"Pretty fair — for me." Mr. Mott nodded, moved off in the direction of the grill, and halted on the outskirts of a loquacious group which was actively engaged in filing demurrers and replications. "Everybody made up?" he inquired genially. With discouraging unanimity they answered in the affirmative; and in the same breath they asked him how he was traveling.

" Not bad — that is, for me," said Mr. Mott. He hailed a lone wayfarer who was hurrying along the aisle. " Anybody looking for an extra man? "

" Sorry! Say, Val, there's a special competition on for the afternoon; heard about it? "

" *No,*" said Mr. Mott, alert. " What is it? "

" Straight medal-play, handicap. Special prize put up by one of the newcomers. Wasn't on the regular program."

" Is that so? I'll have to see about it. Well, how're you hitting 'em? "

" Vile! " The lone man took up his march in the direction of the attendant's room, and Mr. Mott shook his head in profound sympathy, and went on to the bulletin-board, where he delayed for a moment to inspect the current handicap-list. As he stood there, sniffing contemptuously at his own modest rating, a trio of late arrivals burst through the side door, and bore down upon him, laughing and talking and forecasting the future with that incorrigible golfing optimism which is Phœnix-born every day out of the black ashes of yesterday's sodden facts. Mr. Mott knew all three, and he hailed them cheerfully.

" Hello! Looking for a fourth man? "

"No; somebody's waiting for us. No competition this afternoon, is there?"

"Of course there is! Special prize for straight medal-play," said Mr. Mott. "Don't you fellows ever read the announcements?"

"Is that so? That's fine! Thought there wasn't anything doing! Well, how were you going this morning?"

"Oh, pretty fair — for me, of course."

The trio hurried away, and Mr. Mott, lingering only to make sure that the tabular results of the competition for the treasurer's cup still remained on the board,— he hadn't been put out until the semi-finals, and liked to see his name in the bracket, — strolled into the grill, and cast about him for companionship.

The low-studded room, as Mr. Mott entered, echoed the mad confusion of a political convention crossed with a dairy restaurant. Crockery clattered against wooden surfaces, plated silver clattered against crockery, tumblers clinked to tumblers, and hobnails grated on the red-tiled floor. Men in knickerbockers and men in flannels huddled close to the round tables and bawled statistics at one another; men in street clothes dragged rattling caddy-bags through from the office; men flushed and perspiring stamped in from the eighteenth green, and clamored loudly at the bar. Disheveled waiters dodged aimlessly about in answer to the insistence of a dozen members simultaneously. Half a hundred voices swelled in extenuation, alibi, defense; half a hundred voices rang clear in joyous prophecy. Drifting clouds of light-gray smoke clung like a canopy to the ceiling. The atmosphere was surcharged with excitement, and Mr. Mott's nostrils dilated as he scented it. The air quivered to the ungodly tumult, and Mr. Mott's ear-drums vibrated as he heard it.

"Waiter! Hang that waiter! Here, you! I —"

"I had a putt for a forty-seven coming in; without that nine on the tenth I 'd have had a putt for a forty-one —"

"Come on; be a sport; make it a ball Nassau —"

"Why should *I* give you a stroke? Here's *my* suggestion —"

"All right! All right! Count it up yourself! 5, 7, 4, 9, 6, 6, 8 —"

"Five aces in one! *I* 'll stand!"

"Hey, Jim! I had a par five —"

"Waiter! Waiter! I did n't order soup!"

"That 's ground under repair. It says so on the card —"

"Oh, I could n't hit a balloon. Worst I *ever* did!"

"Well, if you start us one up on each nine and —"

"Confound it! *I* did n't make the rules! It costs you two strokes!"

"Telephone! Telephone for Mr. Smithson! Mrs. Smithson calling —"

"Well, my handicap's too low. He's been under ninety twice this year, and the best I ever made in my life was a ninety-four, and still I 've got to give him three strokes —"

"*Waiter!* Hurry along that club sandwich, will you?"

"If you 'd just keep that left shoulder down, Bill, and remember to follow through —"

"I 'll *bet* you I break 110 —"

"Oh, if I could putt, I 'd be all right. I just can't putt."

"Here, give *me* that check! Oh, come now; that 's not right —"

"Then I went all to pieces —"

"Well, if I 'd been playing my game —"

"Honest, I 'd like to play you even, but I have n't touched a club since June —"

"Oh, I was *awful!* — How about you?"

"*Waiter!*"

Mr. Mott smiled happily, and button-holed the chairman of the handicap committee.

" Made up yet? " he inquired.

The chairman was prone to brevity.

" Yes. How 'd you come out this morning? "

" Rotten! " said Mr. Mott, promptly. " Tore up my card; I was fierce. Know anybody that 's looking for a match? "

" Yes, there 's a new member out by the caddy-house. Don't know who he is, but he 's alone. I thought somebody ought to give him a welcome. *You* do it, Val."

" Good idea — I will." Mr. Mott edged his way to the outer door, bellowed over his shoulder to one who had bellowed a question at him — the answer was " Pretty fair — for me! "— and emerged to the gravel walk. At this hour the vicinity of the first tee was deserted, but before the professional's tiny house Mr. Mott saw a lanky stranger dallying in an attitude of longing; Mr. Mott drew near and grinned. The stranger looked up, and presently grinned in return.

" Waiting for somebody? " asked Mr. Mott.

" No," said the stranger. " Just taking my chances; I 'm a new member."

" Indeed! My name 's Mott."

" Chapman 's mine."

They shook hands. Mr. Mott glowed with the consciousness of duty well done.

"I'm alone, too. Suppose we try it?"

"I'd be glad to. Your name up for the handicap?"

"Not yet."

"I'll put it up," volunteered Mr. Mott. In the top space on the ruled sheet tacked to the scoreboard he scrawled his own patronymic, and added his stroke allowance. "What's yours?"

"They haven't given me one. I've been in the club only a week."

"*Well*," said Mr. Mott, uncertainly, "then you can't very well compete —"

"Oh, I'm not going to. I'm not strong for tournaments, anyway. If you don't mind, I'll just attest your round; I'm not in condition anyway."

"All right." Mr. Mott dusted his hands, and stepped over to the caddy-master. "A couple of boys ready? Who do I draw? This one? My bag there? Now, son, your job is to *watch the ball*. You remember that, will you? Let's have the driver." He strode within the fatal inclosure, and swung the club experimentally at a trespassing cigarette stub. The stub leaped forward a yard, accurately on the line. "What do you play around in?"

56

"Oh, I'm erratic," said Chapman, watching intently. "You take the honor, please."

"Well, if you say so." He chuckled. "Might as well take it when I can get it. I may never have another chance." He teed an almost new ball, and took his stance; waggled, hesitated, stooped, glanced at his caddy, and glared at him. "Another ball," he said shortly. "Red-line Silver King out of the pocket." The caddy, overwhelmed with guilt, furnished it. It was of the same brand, the same marking, the same weight, and showed the same degree of wear and tear as the original choice; but Mr. Mott, for reasons comprehended only by golfers, regarded it with far greater satisfaction. It was the ball with which he had made the last hole in a par five on the morning round. It was, so to speak, already broken in, trained, biddable. Mr. Mott teed it, and after swinging once or twice in exaggeratedly correct form, lunged downward savagely.

"Good ball!" approved Chapman.

"Too high," said Mr. Mott, with meretricious disgust. It was the longest drive he had made from the first tee in six weeks.

The stranger hit a prodigious hook out of bounds. On his second attempt the hook was less pronounced; he was in the rough. The two players set out fraternally on their journey.

"Been playing much lately?" inquired Mr. Mott.

"Not a great deal. Only once or twice since April."

"You've got a fine follow-through, though."

"Unfortunately, there's more to the game than that," deprecated Chapman. He selected a spoon, and was hole-high to the left of the green.

"Beautiful! Just a trifle off," commented Mr. Mott. With the sole of his club he patted down a worm-cast; with his heel he deleted a tuft of grass from the complications of his lie. He made his effort, and afterwards he held himself rooted to the spot until he had verified, by three swings at vacancy, his unexpressed opinion that, given another opportunity, he would have split the flag, instead of dubbing fifty feet downhill. "I can't keep my head down," he lamented. "Oh, well —" He turned suddenly to his caddy, and sent a bolt of lightning at him. "*Watch* this one!" he ordered. And the caddy obediently watched it hobble a hundred yards, and disappear among the leaves of a dry trench.

As Mr. Mott, looking aggrievedly at a pair which had come up behind him and were yelling "Fore!" at the top of their lungs, stood on the first green and noted his score, he was impelled to quote history.

"I had a six here this morning," he sighed. "It's a tricky green, is n't it?"

"Very," agreed his partner. "You keep the honor all the way, will you? You're in the tournament, and I'm not."

"Just as you say. On this one you want to aim pretty well to the left of the mound." Mr. Mott drove thirty yards to the right of it. "Doggone it!" he exclaimed, with his hands on his hips, "that club's no earthly good; I can't hit the broad side of a barn with it! It is n't balanced, or something. Further to the left, Mr. Chapman." Here Chapman sent forth a towering drive which at least was out of trouble. "*That's* safe! You're lucky."

"Oh, I'm not kicking," said Chapman placidly. "But I'm afraid you're in the pit."

"I see," said Mr. Mott, getting into his stride, "that that Bobby Jones has n't been doing as well this season as he did last. Well, that's the way it ought to work out. He's too young to have all that success; it might have spoiled him. Besides, the national's no place for a boy like that. I was hoping he would n't go too far at Merion a year ago."

"He made a seventy-four," said Chapman,

59

shrugging his shoulders, " and a seventy-six and a seventy-seven —"

" Oh, that's not so very remarkable. You take these caddies; they watch good players, and get hold of a good swing, and they're not bothered with nerves —"

" Pardon me, but I think you're back there about ten yards, Mr. Mott."

" So I am! Much obliged! Fore!"

Within a quarter of a mile there was no one who might conceivably have been endangered by Mr. Mott's recovery from the sand-pits, but his warning cry was both mechanical and peremptory. He eyed the flag, three hundred yards in advance, and with his eye still on it he played the mashie-niblick in the stroke which made Edward Ray internationally famous. It made Mr. Mott apoplectic. Thenceforward he progressed by slow and circuitous stages to the sloping green, and upon his arrival he was too deeply perturbed to sympathize with Chapman, whose iron shot had found a trap, and whose approach was beyond the hole. To be sure, the sinking of a long putt did much to salve the irritation in Mr. Mott's bosom, and although Chapman also holed a twenty-footer, Mr. Mott secretly felt, and generously withheld the statement, that Chapman had been excessively fortunate in the roll of the green. And he was too much absorbed in his own cosmos to inquire Chapman's score.

The third hole was short; that is, it was short for scratch-players. Mr. Mott had seen Tommy Kerrigan, the club professional, once play it with a heavy mashie; he had seen Sumner Hollander, who, although rated at nine, was Mr. Mott's ideal performer, overplay it with a mid-iron. Therefore Mr. Mott, who, if he could have reached the pin with a full brassey once out of three trials, would have owed sacrifices to the gods and blessings to a beam wind, chose a mid-iron.

"I'm not generally as bad as this," he explained when the ball had found cover in a growth of underbrush. "I'm not getting my wrists into it, that's all. I don't know what's the matter with me to-day. I don't seem to have any snap. It's costing me a stroke a hole, too."

"Easily," said Chapman. He, too, was off the line, but he was near enough to the green to use a putter while Mr. Mott was still flailing at the underbrush, and he was down in four to Mr. Mott's six.

"Now for a long one," complained Mr. Mott, climbing the eminence to the fourth tee. "Well, I suppose I'll have to take that driver of Kerrigan's again. If I had any sense I'd drive with an iron. Well, never mind. I believe in playing the right club. Watch it, boy!" He hit a screaming liner down the alley for more than two hundred precious yards, and posed diligently and without motion, until the ball had not only come to rest, but had also lain quiescent for several seconds. He regarded the club-head in general perplexity. He tested the spring of the shaft. He breathed deeply, and made way for Chapman; and after Chapman, owing to a half-top, had failed by a full rod to equal that drive of Mr. Mott's, he relentlessly fought down the smile which struggled for its outlet. Indeed, he was rather astonishingly severe and unemotional for a man who had just accomplished a praiseworthy feat, and got back on his game. He endeavored by conversation to disguise his glory.

"You've just joined the club, Mr. Chapman?"

"Only a week ago, Mr. Mott."

"Pretty nice course, don't you think? It's very hard. It's harder by three strokes than any other course in the metropolitan district, and the fairway's a bit ragged, and the greens are pretty nearly hopeless; but you wait five years! I tell you, a man's got to keep out of the rough on this course or he's dished. I like a stiff course; it's the only kind to have. Where did you play formerly?"

"Over in Boston — Woodland."

"Oh! Do you know Francis Ouimet?"

"I should say I do! Do *you?*"

"Well, not personally," said Mr. Mott, with some haste. "But of course . . . If he had more time to play, he 'd be a wizard, would n't he? Fore!"

"You 're in the pit!" shrilled Mr. Mott's caddy.

"Well, don't tell me about it *now!*" roared Mr. Mott, turning livid. He glanced at Chapman. "Excuse me, I thought you 'd played. Well, of all the —" He saw Chapman's stinging brassey, which had threatened to sail into a grove of pines to westward, suddenly veer to the east, and drop lazily abaft the green.

"Pretty lucky," said Chapman. "I played for a slice, but —"

"*Lucky!* I wish I had *half* your luck! I 'd be down to a three handicap, by gosh! See my ball anywhere, caddy? You said it was in the pit."

The boy indicated it.

"It bounced over, sir."

"Humph!" said Mr. Mott, accepting the gift of the fates without evident thankfulness. "Well, why don't you *watch* it, boy? Tell me it 's in the pit, and then . . . Stand still, will you? Stop rattling those clubs!" He hit a high iron and lost it in the sun. "Say, I did n't see that one at all."

"Neither did I," said Chapman. "But it sounded like a clean hit."

Mr. Mott shifted the responsibility to his faithful retainer, who was nonchalantly chewing gum.

"Did you mark it, caddy?"

"No, sir; could n't see it drop, Sun 's in my eyes." Mr. Mott snorted, and tossed his cleek to the ground.

"Good Lord!" he snapped. "What d' you think you 're paid for? D' you think I hire you to *lose* balls? Anybody can carry the clubs; your job is to *watch* the *ball!* Why did n't you mark it? That 'll make three I 've lost to-day, and you —"

"It 's on," stated the caddy, chewing rapidly.

"*On!* Where?"

"On the green. Over by the sprinkler."

Mr. Mott coughed delicately, and looked at Chapman under his lashes. Chapman was n't on; Chapman was n't on by a good ten yards, but Mr. Mott was on in three, and the hole was a par five.

"I 've got a chance for a birdie," he whispered to himself, "a chance for a four. It 's four hundred and eighty yards, and I 've got a chance for a four. For a birdie. . . . *Good shot!*" Chapman had clipped up neatly.

Mr. Mott took his putter, and made an awkward jab at the ball. It fled at a disconcerting angle. Mr. Mott flushed, pursued the gutty, and jabbed again. Then he lifted himself erect, and poured out into the world the offscourings of his innermost soul. He reviled himself, the Silver King golf-ball, the Vaile putter, the greenskeeper, the turf, the contour of the land, the Scotch who had invented the game, and the promoters who had organized the club. As an afterthought, he hurled the putter into a convenient hazard, and, seizing the first weapon which came to hand,— a niblick,— struck so fair and true that the ball went down for a six, one over par.

"Too bad!" said Chapman. "I missed an easy one, myself."

"I had a chance for a four," declared Mr. Mott, loudly. "Of all the rotten putting I ever saw in my *life* that was the worst! On the green in three, and three putts! These greens are rotten! Worst in the world; and believe me, I've seen some bad ones! Where's my driver? Hurry up, there!"

While his mood was of grim resolution, and he concentrated rigidly upon the act, he drove off in excellent form and with highly creditable results.

"There!" he ejaculated. "*Now* I'm getting back on my game. That old war-club certainly does poke 'em out when I hit 'em right. But three putts, and only one over par at that! If our greens were as good as they've got at Wykagyl or Sleepy Hollow —"

65

IF YOU DON'T MIND MY TELLING YOU

He observed that his companion had again
hooked, and by virtue of his own superiority of direction he was vastly exhilarated. The second
shots, too, filled him with passionate joy, for he was
safely over the brook, while Chapman had pulled
into tall grass. Mr. Mott sidled toward his
partner, and made diplomatic overtures of assistance.

"If you don't mind my telling you," he said,
"you stand too far back of the ball. You can't
help hooking when you do that. You push the
face of the club right across the ball. It's like a
massé shot in billiards. You're getting good distance, but you hook all the time. Just straighten
'em out and you'll be 'way out every time. Stand
farther ahead, and you'll be all right."

"I certainly am hooking 'em," acknowledged the
lanky man.

"Well, if you don't mind my telling you —"

"Not a bit!"

"More like this," said Mr. Mott, illustrating.
"Go back slower, and let go with your right hand
at the top of the swing. Then take hold hard with
your left when you start to come down. It's the
left hand that does the business. And follow
through more. Now, you take that last shot of
mine; I hit three inches behind the ball, and the

66

follow through saved it. All of it was bad but the follow through; but what happened? It went as straight as a die. Say, are those people going to stay on that green all *night?* Fore!"

"Oh, they have n't holed out yet."

"Yes, they have; they 're counting their scores. Some people don't realize there 's such a thing as etiquette in this game. *Fore!*"

He topped into the brook.

"Fore!" said Mr. Mott, waving his niblick.

He hammered the ball into a bank of yielding clay.

"Fore!" rasped Mr. Mott, setting his teeth.

He essayed a pitching stroke, a lofting stroke, an extricating stroke, and two shoveling strokes, and the last of these brought him to solid earth.

"Fore!" shouted Mr. Mott, wild-eyed. He ran an approach to the edge of the green and panted violently. "Four — and I 'm on in five," said Mr. Mott, utterly innocent. "Where 'd *you* go?"

"Just off — over by the water-pipe."

Mr. Mott exhaled luxuriously, and fanned himself with his hat.

"That is n't bad. One of you boys take the flag. Good work!" Secretly he held that Chapman's run-up was a fearful fluke.

"Sink it now," urged Chapman, encouragingly.

67

Mr. Mott tried his best to sink it, and missed by a bare inch.

"Throw that back here!" he ordered.

The second endeavor was flawless. Legally, Mr. Mott had taken two putts; morally, he had taken one — the last one. It was this consciousness of innate ability, this realization that if he had aimed a hair's-breadth farther to the left he would have sunk the first attempt that cheered and inspired him. He could have done it if he had really cared about it. And Chapman missed a two-footer!

"If you don't mind my telling you," said Mr. Mott, with admirable restraint, "you can putt a whole lot better if you turn the face of your putter over toward the hole. It puts a drag on the ball. It makes it run close to the ground. I had a six; no, seven. That first one should have gone down. Seven."

"Twelve," said his caddy, apprehensive, but judicial.

Mr. Mott turned upon him vehemently.

"*Twelve!* What in thunder are you talking about? Five on the green —"

"No, sir, ten —"

"Listen! Three in the brook,—" Mr. Mott's mouth opened slowly, and his jaw fell,—"three in the brook," he repeated in horror, "and —"

"And nine out, sir. You yelled 'Fore!' and counted the next stroke five —"

"Give me the mid-iron," said Mr. Mott, abruptly. "Get down there and mark this shot!" He wheeled to gaze at the scene of his recent dredging operations. "Three in the brook, four, five, six, seven — *Hey! Stop swinging those clubs!* Well, I *said* it was seven! Three in the brook —"

"Your honor, Mr. Mott."

"Thank you." He teed for the short sixth across a threatening ravine. "*Caddy!* wake up there!" He turned to his partner with a gesture of Christian resignation. "Don't you wish," he asked, "that just once in a while you'd find a caddy that showed some *interest* in the game?"

The sixth hole was a trifling matter of a hundred and fifty yards; but to render it attractive to experts, there were mental, physical, and psychological hazards cunningly placed by nature, aided and abetted by Donald Ross. As Mr. Mott wavered on the tee, he saw a deep gully, weed-infested and spotted with frowning rocks; he saw pits limiting and guarding the green; he saw trees and excavations and a stone wall. Upon its misshapen mound of sand he saw the Silver King waiting resignedly for its certain punishment. He saw his mid-iron, broad bladed and heavy, a club capable of propelling thirty pennyweight of rubber and silk an eighth of a mile and more if properly coerced. Yet Mr. Mott discounted the inherent qualities of that iron, just as he discounted the elasticity of the golf-ball and the power of his wrists and forearms. He recalled that on the last few occasions of his attack upon this hole he had shafted his ball over the stone wall, and he wondered dumbly how he might prevent a repetition of the error. Instinct warned him to go for the hole, and play with assurance; but for several minutes he had n't been on good terms with his instinct. He struggled to revive the warnings of those who have written text books, to remember what Taylor or Braid or Travers has prescribed as antidotes for shafting tee-shots. "Stop talking!" he growled at the caddies. "How d' you think I can drive when you 're talking!" Out of the obscurity of printed words a phrase flashed to his brain and he was aware that as Haultain says, he was about to pivot on the head of the left thigh-bone, working in the cotyloidal cavity of the *os innominatum*. He placed the mid-iron in position, and told himself that upon his life he was n't to move his right gastrocnemius or sartorius except torsionally. He rehearsed, in one mad instant,

platitudes affecting the right elbow, the eyes, the
left knee, the interlocking grip, and the distribu-
tion of weight. He lifted the club stiffly, and
brought it down again. Too cramped! He settled
himself more comfortably, and peered at the stone
wall. The green, half bathed in golden sunshine,
half purplish in dense shadow, seemed to reach out
yearning arms to draw the Silver King to its broad
bosom. A hundred and fifty yards, par three. Mr.
Mott caught his breath in a quick intake, and drove
sickeningly into the stone wall.

"Oh, tough!" said Chapman.

But the features of Mr. Mott expressed no rage.
On the contrary, he was smiling placidly, as a parent
smiles at a wayward child. The crisis had come
and gone; the most difficult obstacle of the entire
round was now a matter of indifference to him; he
had known positively that he was destined somehow to entangle himself with that stone wall, and
now he had done it. Even so, he did n't begrudge
his partner that arching shot which spanned the
ravine, and lacked not more than a yard or two of
carrying the green; on the contrary, he was glad
that Chapman had done so well.

"I *always* dub this hole," he said cheerfully. "I
got a two on it last July, but ordinarily I'm satisfied if I get a four. You're well up there; still a

tiny bit of a hook, though. But you 're doing a lot better since I told you."

"I 'm working hard enough to straighten 'em out," deprecated Chapman.

"Well, if you take a nice, easy swing, and don't pull your body round, you 'll get good results. I hope you don't mind my telling you."

"Far from it," said Chapman, humbly.

Mr. Mott's caddy pointed to the ball, which was virtually unplayable among the stones. Mr. Mott, now that he had passed the climax of his round, was suddenly dogged and determined. It was all well enough to flub the drive, but this approach of his was serious business. He broke off a reed or two which interfered with his stance; he commandeered both caddies to assist him in the removal of sundry large rocks; he bent the grasses so that he had a fighting chance to smash through with his deep-faced mashie. Down on the green Chapman was watching earnestly. On the sixth tee a fast-moving foursome was emitting comments which blew across the ravine, and caused the muscles of Mr. Mott's jaw to tighten significantly. Duffer, was he! He 'd show 'em whether he was a duffer or not! He focused on the flag, and swung the mashie in a wide ellipse.

Mr. Mott, by virtue of that mysterious and

extraordinary sense with which some men are sometimes gifted, had known with utter privity of knowledge that he was sure to recover from the rough.
There was no doubt about it; it was his destiny.
What he had n't known, or remotely suspected, was
that he would cover sixty good yards with that clean
swipe, and lose his ball in the wilderness of the ad-
jacent jungle. And even in that moment when he
most commiserated with himself for the gross
faultiness of the club and the grave defects of the
ball, he was n't nearly so much tortured by the necessity of playing three, still from trouble, as he was
by the necessity of allowing that cynical foursome
to go through. His gorge rose at the mere conception of being passed; in match-play he would have
conceded the hole instanter rather than suffer the
ignominy of signaling a foursome to take prece-
dence; but in medal-play he must finish every hole
and hole every putt; so that he fretted impatiently
for five long minutes, spoke to his caddy in curt
monosyllables, and majestically expelled from the
course, as a thief and a pirate, a soiled and tattered
renegade who leaned over the wall and offered to
sell him two second-hand floaters for a quarter. In
days gone by Mr. Mott had bought perhaps two
dozen balls from that self-same urchin, that boy
who wearily spent the long summer evenings in

beating thicket and brush for abandoned gutties; but to-day he looked askance upon the scoundrel, and saw him plainly for what he was, a trafficker in illicit wares, a golf-hound outlawed and thrice condemned. Besides, last Saturday Mr. Mott had purchased four old balls from him only to discover later that two of them were balls which Mr. Mott himself had lost a fortnight ago. They had his initials on them.

The foursome, completing their routine with incredible speed and skill, disappeared in the middle distance. Mr. Mott played three, and Mr. Mott played four, and if he had n't kept majestic control over his temper, he would have dumped his clubs in the nearest pit, brained his caddy with a patent putter, and started incoherently for Bloomingdale. As it was, he merely confirmed the theory that the terminology of masculine hysteria is limited to four suffixes, and played five without caring whether he found the hole or Long Island Sound. As a matter of fact, he found the hole.

"Bully!" said Chapman. "I made mine, too; thought we 'd better save time. I putted while you were hunting."

Mr. Mott, red and perspiring, shook his head sadly.

"I ought to have had a four," he maintained.

74

But to-day he looked mercilessly upon the scoundrel, and saw him
for what he was, a trafficker in illicit wares

"I wasted a shot. That's eight strokes I've absolutely thrown away this round. I ought to have had a four-easy. If you don't mind my telling you, you'd better play straight for the big tree. Then your hook 'll make it come around into the fair." Whereupon Mr. Mott hit a very high, very short hook, and as he postured in the guise of Ajax,— save that Ajax presumably had no such costume and no such implement to intensify the dramatic value of his gestures,— he fervently apostrophized the wind, which had taken a perfectly straight ball and blown it into a trap. He wasn't influenced in his decision by the sight of a marker-flag drooping lazily on its staff, nor by the circumstance that Chapman's drive, which attained almost equal height, came to earth without a single degree of deviation from the line of shortest distance.

"The wind took it right around!" flamed Mr. Mott, snatching his niblick. *"Fore!"*

It was a good out, and Mr. Mott played a goodly third. His fourth, however, was abortive, although the divot flew gracefully. Mr. Mott withheld his analysis until Chapman had curved an approach within striking distance of the green, and then his finer sensibilities prompted him to disregard himself and to tutor Chapman.

"That was a nice ball," he began sincerely, "but

77

you're still hooking. Why don't you try addressing it with the heel of the club? That makes you
come around in after it. You try that, and see
what it does. And I've noticed you go back too
fast. You can't do that and keep your balance unless you're a good player. Slow back, and crook
your left knee more. In at the ball, I mean. Like
this!" His delsarte was masterly; and although he
foundered the shot, the ball rolled and rolled until
it trickled on to the green and stopped dead.
"Well, that's the idea, but I didn't get it up
enough," said Mr. Mott with decent reserve. Subsequently they each used the putter twice.

The eighth was a respite, and they halved it in
four. On the ninth tee, to the frank annoyance of
another foursome which had overtaken them, Mr.
Mott refused to drive until the quartet ahead had
left the green, two hundred and twenty-two yards
away, uphill.

"A good wallop 'll carry that far sometimes,"
he explained with dignity. "I've done it myself.
Almost did it this morning. They're off now,
anyway." Before proceeding to the shot, he condescended to lighten the situation with a ray of humor.
"I'd hate to kill anybody," he said, and after an
enormous swing topped not more than a mallet's
length into the tall grass.

From the restive foursome a gruff voice struck harshly upon Mr. Mott's sensitive ears:

" Well, that was a damn' humane impulse all right! "

With a medal score of sixty-three for the first nine, Mr. Mott bade farewell to all thought of a silver trophy for his library, and devoted himself to a keen study of ballistics as exemplified by his partner's chronic hook. For two holes he fairly exuded advice and encouragement, but at the twelfth tee he was staggered to discover that he had counseled an ingrate. Without question, Chapman was improving steadily; the hook was appreciably less, and Mr. Mott had merely said, with the kindest of motives, that Chapman *was* improving, and that if he 'd only remember to stare while he counted three at the spot where the ball had rested before he hit it, he 'd do even better. And Chapman, smiling faintly, replied in a gentle tone which contained rebuke:

" Perhaps if you 'll play your own game, Mr. Mott, and let me play mine, we 'll get along well enough as it is."

Mr. Mott would n't have been human if he had n't taken seven on the next hole, and he would n't have been human if he had n't experienced a thrill of primitive triumph when Chapman not only hooked his drive, but also his full mid-iron. Granted that his approach was moderately efficient, Chapman deserved nothing better than a seven, or possibly a six, with divine aid; but when he putted wretchedly off direction, and the ball, obviously deflected by the agency of a slope which Mr. Mott had n't seen and could n't discern curled sharply in toward the cup, and tottered to the lip of it, and dropped, Mr. Mott compressed his lips and said nothing. He realized that comment was superfluous; when a man had that sort of luck, which simply compensated for two earlier mistakes, there was nothing for a righteously indignant opponent to say. Chapman had even forfeited his earlier right to be joked about it.

But when Chapman achieved a perfect drive on the thirteenth Mr. Mott burst with information.

" That 's the queerest thing I ever saw in my life! "

" What is? "

" Why, that ball was straight as a die! And you stood for another hook! "

" No! " said Chapman.

" But — why, certainly you did. I 'd have told you, but you 'd begun your swing, and I was afraid of spoiling your shot. It 's the funniest thing I ever saw! Where am I, caddy? "

" In the pit," said the stolid caddy.

By the time he got out, he perceived that his companion had finished, and was sitting on the bench in the shade. Highly offended at the discourtesy, Mr. Mott whistled as a demonstration of independence, and utilized an unconscionable length of time in a study of topography. To do him justice, he was n't seeking to retaliate; he was resolved that by his own excellence in the short game he would display his lack of nerves and his imperturbability in a trying moment. The man whose partner has played out rather than to wait politely while sand-pits are under exploration is subject to an adjustment of poise; and although Mr. Mott had the satisfaction of leaving no loophole for criticism, and of holing prettily, he was nevertheless too fundamentally introspective to drive well on the dog-leg fourteenth.

Furthermore, although the region immediately surrounding his ball was n't placarded as ground under repair when Mr. Mott began his onslaught upon the turf, it was indubitably in need of repair when Mr. Mott got through with it. He quarried out a blanket of gravelly soil at each of four desperate offensives, and when he toiled wearily up the hillside to the rolling green he took two putts for a nine, and was aware that Chapman, whether befriended or betrayed by fortune, hook or no hook, had beaten him by a margin of many strokes.

But the sun was setting, the end was near, and Chapman was a new member. Mr. Mott relaxed somewhat, tore his tournament score-card to bits, and scattered them on the grass.

"No use keeping *that* any more," he said. "I can't putt on these plowed fields they call greens. They're a disgrace to the club, that's what they are. Now, this is what I call a beautiful hole. Four hundred and sixty — over beyond the farthest line of trees. Par five; it ought to be par six."

"Why?"

Mr. Mott was mildly astonished.

"Because it's a hard hole."

"But par's arbitrary, Mr. Mott."

"Yes, but the greens committee —"

"The greens committee has n't anything to do with it. Any hole up to two hundred and fifty is par three, from that to four fifty is par four, from four fifty-one to six hundred is par five. So this is a par five — and it's only ten yards too long to be a par four."

Mr. Mott blinked at the sun.

"What makes you think that?"

"I don't think it; I *know* it. The U. S. G. A.

changed the figures in April, but the ruling did n't affect this particular distance at that."

" Well, I may be wrong, but my impression is that the greens committee fixes the par for the different holes. Anyway, here goes! "

" Nice ball! " said Chapman.

Mr. Mott smiled conciliatingly.

" Tommy Kerrigan made that driver for me," he said. " It 's a pippin. As soon as I swing I can *feel* I 'm going to hit it clean. I *beg* your pardon! Did I take your mind off your shot? "

" Not at all. I 'm out there about where you are."

" It was a screamer," said Mr. Mott, unaware of the inference to be drawn from the compliment. " As good a drive as I 've seen in a month."

To his immense gratification, he was hole-high on his second shot, and home on his third. He compelled himself to plan for two putts, to insure himself a par five instead of risking all on a bold steal which might prove, by metamorphosis, to be a gift to the devil. In consequence he very nearly holed out, and he was far too enraptured to care what Chapman got. Chapman had manhandled his chip shot, and Mr. Mott had n't noticed the others. Let Chapman account for himself. Par five! Who cared what Chapman got?

According to the custom duly laid down in such cases, Mr. Mott took many practice swings on the sixteenth tee. Temporarily, he had struck his head upon the stars, and with the pride of a champion he swung with a champion's ease and freedom. Par five! Mr. Mott, with the image of victory statue hovering before his eyes, clipped bits of turf from the scarred tee and ogled the green. Kerrigan had often overdriven it; once when the ground was baked out; it wasn't much more than two hundred and forty yards. And the rough directly before the tee, the trap to the left, and the rough to the right, what were they? Who but novices were to be alarmed by puny obstacles such as these? Surely not the man who has made the long fifteenth in a par five!

"Fore!" he said mechanically.

Mr. Mott drove magnificently, and started hastily over the foot-bridge, then halted at the pleasant laughter of his companion, and shamefacedly stood aside. He never looked to see where Chapman drove; his consciousness was riveted upon a small white object far up on the slope. And since, during his walk, he told himself exactly how he should play his approach, how he should stand, how he should swing, he later stood and swung without destructive uncertainty, and so pitched fairly to the pin. The putt was simple; Mr. Mott achieved it without a tremor.

"Three!" he whispered to himself. "One under par! One under par for two holes! Gosh! If I had n't been so rotten up to the fifteenth I'd have had a chance!" Aloud, he said: "Par four's too much for this hole. It ought to be three. What was yours?"

"Four," said Chapman. "Your approach was too good; it was a wonder."

"Pure wrist shot. Notice how I took the club back? Sort of scoop the ball up — pick it up clean? That's what I've been working for — pick 'em up clean with lots of back spin. You get that by sort of sliding under the ball. Well, two more to go!"

"Let's make 'em good!" adjured Chapman.

"One under par for two holes," thought Mr. Mott, slashing a low drive to the open. "Say, I guess somebody would n't turn up his nose at that, eh? A five and a three! I was — let's see — thirty-eight for five holes, and a five and a three make forty-six. Oh, I beg your pardon!" He was wool-gathering squarely in front of Chapman, who presently put a hooked ball somewhat beyond Mr. Mott's. "My! what a wonderful day for golf!" said Mr. Mott, enthusiastically. "Not a breath of wind, not too hot, just right."

"It suits me. You got a nice drive there."

"Too high," said Mr. Mott. He played a jumping shot which ran briskly over the shallow pit guarding the green, and came to a standstill not twenty feet from the cup. He putted, and was dead. He holed out with neatness and precision, and knew that he had beaten Chapman by a stroke. "Gad, what a green!" said Mr. Mott, pop-eyed. "Like a billiard-table. We've got an English greenskeeper here; he's a wonder. Best greenskeeper in the East. Sleepy Hollow and Pine Valley have nothing on *us*."

"You're finishing strong, Mr. Mott. Go to it!"

"One under par for three holes," shouted Mr. Mott's dual personality to Mr. Mott. "And — how many am I to here?" To Chapman he said, "I'm trying to remember — what did I have on the tenth?"

"Six," said Chapman.

"Why, are you sure?"

"Positive."

"Well, I *thought* I remembered it was six,— I've been counting up,— but —"

"I can name every stroke you've played since you started," said Chapman. "It gets to be second nature after a while. It's only a knack; but

86

sometimes it's very valuable. I know every shot we've *both* played."

Mr. Mott looked doubtful.

"I'd take the short end of a sizable bet on that proposition. What was my fourth shot on the fourth hole?"

"Brassey to the green," said Chapman. "You got a six."

"Well, I'll be — what did I make on the seventh hole?"

"Seven."

"Well, what was my third shot on the tenth?"

"Just a minute — why, it was a topped mashie into the trap. You were on in four and down in six."

Mr. Mott prepared to drive.

"Do you always remember scores like that?"

"Always."

Mr. Mott drove far down the fairway. Exalted and emboldened, he ventured to explain briefly just how he had done it. Then when Chapman had hit a long, low ball which developed a faint hook as it dipped to the hollows, Mr. Mott was constrained to offer condolence.

"If you just get that kink out of your shots you'll play under a hundred," he stated flatly. "Under a hundred with no trouble at all."

His companion chuckled involuntarily.

" Well, I hope I should."

" Nothing in the world but too much wrist action. Look! You don't see *me* hooking many balls, do you? Watch how I get my wrists into this one!" He was unerring on the line, and Chapman nodded understandingly.

" You could n't ask anything better than that."

" And the best of it is," said Mr. Mott, glowing, "that I always know what's the matter with me. I was n't always that way; there was a time when I was way up in the air about it, so I know just how you feel. Now go after this one! Easy — and follow through! Oh — too bad!"

Chapman, however, was n't overly discouraged.

" It's safe, is n't it?"

" Yes, it's almost up on the brook; but if you'd gone into the woods, it would have been a lost ball. *This* way!" Mr. Mott illustrated once more. " Here she goes!" And he made his third consecutive shot which was without reproach.

Chapman, however, hooked a trifle even with his full mashie, which was barely off the green, and Mr. Mott sighed for him. For himself, he ran up alongside. If he could go down in two more, he would have played the last four holes in par! Mr. Mott reached for his putter, and fumbled with it. He bent over the ball, and observed that it was smaller than he had suspected; he told himself that he should have chosen a larger size. Mr. Mott's lips formed the word "Fore!" and he tapped impotently. The ball rolled in, swerved, struck a transient leaf, and Mr. Mott, his mind erased of any conception of a partner, or of the etiquette of the links, dashed forward. Two feet to the cup, two feet for a six, and the last four holes in par! Fifty-one for the last nine — his record! Mr. Mott, gasping, clutched the putter, and struck, and heard the click of the contact, and saw a cylindrical abyss, lined with zinc, open wide to receive the Silver King. He stood up, choked with emotion.

"The — last four holes in — in *par!*" he faltered.

"Hold the flag, boy!" said Chapman.

Mr. Mott watched, fascinated. Inwardly he knew, before Chapman putted, that the stroke was too light; and as the lanky stranger strolled up for further trial, Mr. Mott, in his terrific success, blurted out his final charge.

"If you don't mind my telling you," he said, "rest your right hand on your knee, and —"

The ball rattled into the cup. From a camp-chair under the awning a member of the Board of Governors rose and sauntered toward them.

"Mr. Chapman!" said Mr. Mott. He offered his hand across the hole.

"Thank you, Mr. Mott." Chapman's clasp was convincing.

"I was par for the last four holes! If I'd only got back on my game sooner! Listen! If you did n't hook so much —"

"Yes?" The voice of the stranger was dull with weariness.

"Well, you saw what *I* did! I came back in fifty-one, and the last four in par! Why, if you can play an even game with me *now* —"

"Hello, Chap," said the Governor at his elbow. "How are you going?"

"Fine!" said Mr. Mott, answering for him. "If he only did n't hook so much! How *did* we come out? I was a hundred and fourteen, and you —"

"Eighty-one," said Chapman. "Not bad for a starter." His tone was utterly serious; he was n't jesting.

Mr. Mott's eyes widened. His mouth sagged. A spot of color appeared above his cheek-bones.

"Why, that 's impossible. That 's —"

"Forty-one for first nine, and forty for the last."

Mr. Mott shook as though with palsy, and the putter fell from his hands. He had ignored Chapman's medal score, but now he was recalling incident after incident which seemed to suggest that Chapman had made recoveries, and got distance, and dropped occasional putts. . . .

" Why . . . why . . . I thought we were going about even! "

" Count 'em up," said Chapman, soberly. " 6, 5, 4, 5, 5, 3, 4, 4, 5; is n't that forty-one? 5, 4, 4, 2, 6, 5, 4, 5, 5; is n't that forty? "

" You — you did n't get — a two on the thirteenth! "

" Certainly I did. I holed out while you were in the pit."

Mr. Mott now that he flogged his memory for the facts, seemed dimly to recognize that even those swerving shots of Chapman's had gone off smoothly, and that Chapman had approached sweetly, and putted with distinction. But an eighty-one! And he had volunteered to coach this man; he had showed him in detail how various shots should be made; he had claimed the privilege of instructing a stranger who had hit hardly a straight ball, and still scored close to eighty.

" Wh — what 's your handicap? " he stammered. " You — you are n't *that* Chapman — are you? "

The Governor put his arm over the shoulders of the lanky stranger.

"He had three in New England," he said, "but in the Met. I suppose they'll give him four. How were *you* going, Mr. Mott?"

"Oh, pretty fair — for me," said Mr. Mott, feebly.

But when, bathed and ennobled by fresh linen, he left the clubhouse his heart was once more proud and high. Now and then, to be sure, he experienced a spasm of mortification at the ridiculous figure he had cut before Chapman; nevertheless he was sustained and soothed by the remembrance of the last nine holes in fifty-one and the last four in par. He felt a sturdy manhood, confident and unafraid. To-day he had scored a hundred and fourteen; to-morrow it might be that he, too, should play the full round as he had played the last four holes to-day; upon such dreams is founded the wealth of the club-makers and the athletic outfitters. Timidity in the presence of hazards had gone from him, he believed, forever. Timidity on the greens was a thing of the past. If he could lower his average to a hundred and five by the end of the season,— and with four holes in par to-day he could conceivably do five in par next Saturday, or perhaps as many as six or seven,— he might get down to, say, ninety by next year. If a slim built Bostonian with no style to speak of could approximate eighty, why not Mr. Mott? If a man with a chronic hook could merit a four handicap, why not Mr. Mott? He saw roseate visions of himself at scratch; Walter Travis was already middle-aged before *he* took up the game.

"The last four in par!" whispered Mr. Mott as he went up the steps of his house.

"*Well*," said Mrs. Mott, pathetically, as she came to greet him, "was it worth a thousand dollars to you, Val, to stay away *all* this lovely afternoon?"

"Every cent of it!" cried Mr. Mott, hilariously. "Say, let's motor up the road somewhere; want to? Let's have dinner out! Here, I know! We'll run up to Tumble Inn. Get the Smithsons, and we'll have a party."

"I thought you said you couldn't go out to-night!" She was frankly suspicious.

"Rot! I never said that, did I? Must have been a slip of the tongue. Call the Smithsons, will you?"

"It *must* have been worth while, your staying," said Mrs. Mott, brightening.

"Well, it was," said Mr. Mott. "And I got the last four holes in par! Hurry up and telephone!"

And as he waited for her report, the man who had played a hundred and fourteen stood before the long mirror in the hallway, and gripped an imaginary club, and swung it, and finished gloriously, with the body well twisted and the hands close to the neck, and grinned happily at the reflection of another champion in the making. For this is at once the faith and the hope, the Credo and the Te Deum of the golfer of all time and of whatever ability,— Thank God for to-morrow!

THE RUNNER-UP

THE quinquennium must have had carte-blanche in its battle with Harrower, for he had changed amazingly. In fact, when we first saw him climbing out of a taxicab at the Country Club veranda, we did n't recognize him at all. We looked at him incuriously, and by-and-by Starbuck remarked that there was a face that only a mother could love. It wore the anxious expression of a man who has just broken his midiron in a medal play. Even when he came up to us, and registered exuberant delight, and quite spontaneously called Starbuck and me by name, we were n't quite certain whether he was a process-server, or merely an acquaintance of some distant relation of ours who had told him to look us up when he was near New York and we 'd see that he had a good time.

" You remember me, don't you? " he asked, with that quizzical pleasantry which, in making the other fellow uneasy, is comparable with the small-town joke of insisting that somebody else guess who 's on the telephone.

Starbuck, bluffing nobly, said: "Why should n't we?"

Then there was a fearful silence, which endured until some one tactlessly snickered. That was what broke up the meeting. Ten minutes later we were all down in the grill talking at once, and Harrower was trying to show the steward how they make a Bronx cocktail with pineapple juice in Honolulu; and Henderson had already mentioned several times the good golf he had played three weeks ago Saturday; and Starbuck and I had agreed that, except for his hair, complexion, and mustache, Harrower looked just as he had five years before, and that we 'd have known him instantly if he 'd only taken his hat and glasses off. But that was primarily to hearten and encourage Harrower. As a matter of fact, he had changed so that not one of us would have recognized him.

Now, there are only three reasons — three logical and sufficient reasons — why a man of twenty-seven should make a pilgrimage to the town of his youth after all his family have moved away; but it was n't until we had finished our reminiscences at the club, and Harrower had come over to dine with me at the Inn, that I discovered his reason to be the third. Indeed, the delay was n't creditable; for, according

to his own declaration, he had n't come back to daz-
zle Pomfret with the brilliance of his achievements
— he admitted that he had achieved nothing — and
he had no intention of buying the old homestead
as a keepsake and transmutendum. Nevertheless,
my stupidity continued as far as the salad; when
after inquiring about every one else in the bailiwick
he asked entirely too casually, far too indifferently,
how Margaret Ashton was getting along — if she
were married yet; if she were more or less beautiful than formerly; if she were engaged; if I thought
that she would remember him.

I said that she was unmarried, though happy;
that she was generally considered more or less beautiful; that her health provided no source of revenue
to the medical profession. And at that instant I
knew very accurately what had brought Harrower
back home; and I was sorry that he had wasted his
time. Ahead of him there were half a dozen candi-
dates, including Jimmy Starbuck, who was popularly supposed to be the leader.

"I have n't laid my eyes on her," he said reflectively, " since just before I left for Cambridge
for senior year. Curious how things happen, is n't
it? One Christmas I sent her four dozen American
Beauties, and she sent me a chased silver cigarette-
case; and the year after that she sent me a card with

holly on it, and I sent her one with poinsettias. I wonder if I ought to go up to call?"

"If you did n't come out here to see all your old friends," I said, "what *did* you come for? To wear out your old clothes?"

As nearly as I could judge from his reply, which was heavily loaded with superfluous explanations, he had run out from New York for the primary purpose of vegetating in Pomfret for a day while he embraced with his soul the region of his birth. He would reflect upon the advantages which would obtain if he were able to shatter the material world to bias, and remold it in accordance with his practical experience. He would be stirred again by the emotions of that period during which it was still prophesied that he was "going to be successful."

"Of course," he finished, "there are a few old friends I 'd like to drop in on —"

"Up on the hill," I told him, "the dropping in is pretty good any evening after nine. Why don't we go up?"

"Go up? Go up to the Ashtons?" He was astonishingly excited about it.

"Why not? I thought you 'd like it."

He looked at me as though I had given him a pass to paradise.

"Well, I *should* like it — that is, if you 'd telephone beforehand — I expect to come out again soon, you know — she *might* not —"

"Telephone nothing!" I said. "Peggy does n't faint easily, and we can walk it in fifteen minutes." I swung him relentlessly toward the doorway, and he resisted very little. "It 'll be good exercise." Our hats were on the rack; we went down the steps together.

"You know," said Harrower, apropos of nothing whatsoever, "when a man comes back to the scenes of his childhood he ought to have *something* to show for the time he 's been away. Why, it 's five solid years! Sixty months! Nearly two thousand days! Think of it! I was twenty-one; and you were twenty-two; and Peggy Ashton was younger than either of us —"

"She is yet," I advised him. But humor had left him, and he was unresponsive.

"When I used to go up this same way every night," he remembered, "I wore tennis shoes, and carried pumps in my pocket — I used to stop in the summer-house to change. It 's still dusty, is n't it? I suppose we *could* have stopped for a shine —"

From the Station Road, we turned up the hill to the left. He recalled that, as a boy, he had turned the same way when going in the same direction, and seemed thrilled at the coincidence. A stone wall, a

clump of larches, a clearing where violets had grown
—all these affected him with memories, running
chiefly to pronouns and adjectives. He had forgotten what was the purport of the recollections, but
the loss of subject-matter did n't disturb him. Subsequently, as we came within sight of the Ashtons'
lawn, he spoke at length without saying anything;
and by this time I realized that, although we had set
out in company, only one of us was really going to
call on Peggy Ashton. I was n't disappointed; Harrower had earned his occasion; and Peggy's father,
for a 27-handicap man, talked golf amazingly
well. I was always glad to spend an evening with
him.

For a few moments we had been aware of a
motor laboring up the steep grade behind us. Now,
as a small and glisteningly new car struggled
abreast, we saw that it contained two passengers —
a very young man who was apathetically inert, and
a girl who was driving. From the forward pitch
of her shoulders, and the strained tenseness of her
whole attitude, she appeared intent on assisting the
car with all her strength in adding to its motive
power the stimulus of personal effort; but, in spite
of this gratuitous moral support, the engine took
suddenly to pounding in outrage at the overload.

"It's going to stall!" gasped the girl. "I *know* it's going to stall!'

"It's going to stall!" gasped the girl. "I *know* it's going to stall!"

"Shift!" said her companion calmly; and, when the motor gulped once more and relapsed into silence thirty yards ahead, he added without particular emphasis or passion: "Bonehead!"

Instinct advised me to loiter. The girl was Peggy Ashton; and something told me that Harrower, within ten minutes, could meet her under infinitely better auspices. The characterization with which she had just been adorned wasn't altogether the prettiest attribute to stop up a hiatus of five years in a romantic acquaintanceship. Somehow, one doesn't center the highest quality of romance in boneheads, even if the appellation isn't merited by the facts. So that I loitered; and when the car had sprung into life again, and curved around the next bend, Harrower looked at me as if I had befriended him. For once in my life, I had encountered a man who instantly sensed and appreciated a finesse.

"Wasn't that Peggy?" he demanded. "Who was the man with her?"

"Her kid brother," I assured him. "Don't you remember little Teddy Ashton?"

"Oh!" said Harrower, and he laughed cheerfully. "That's so — he must be almost grown-up!"

"Eighteen — he 's a great boy! I thought you 'd rather wait for a little more formality —"

"*Much* rather — thanks. So that was Ted, was it?"

"One of the best sports I know — he 's a fine golfer."

"Good, is he?"

"Well," I said, "I 've never heard him swear more than four times in any eighteen holes, and that was one of his very worst days. Does n't *that* convey some idea to you?"

We turned into the driveway. Across the lawn we could see the shimmer of a white dress and of white flannels under the trees; we could see wicker chairs placed to catch the transient breeze from the Sound; we could see the vignette of a maid's uniform moving from the house; we could hear the tinkle of ice against thin glass. Harrower put his arm through mine with the easy camaraderie of our school days.

"It 's great up here," he said. "Is n't it? What 's the commuting time?"

I think Harrower was in love with Peggy from the instant he touched her hand and made the startling comment that it was several years since they had met. And the novelty of the situation rose, not from the perfectly normal circumstance that here

104

was another suitor come to enroll for Peggy Ashton, but rather from the fact that contrary to the usual procedure, when he had been thinking of her for five years, and wondering about her, and letting it go at that, she was at the time of his return neither married to a villain nor indifferent to Harrower. To judge from externals, the stars had been shining, and the breeze had been blowing, and the girl had been waiting across all five of those barren years. And presently Ted Ashton and I finding that the conversation wasn't exactly suited to our moods, went down to the garage, to the room he had fitted up for indoor golf practice on rainy days; and there we discussed all sorts of situations and extraordinary shots, and told each other golf stories, and we could even have tried a stroke or two off the cocoanut matting if Peggy's dog hadn't been sleeping on it.

Harrower and I got to the Inn at half past eleven. He had planned to go back to New York that night, but now, especially since the last train had gone, he admitted that he had better spend the night with me. The next morning, after he had telephoned to town, and found that there was nothing important enough to require his presence, he consented to spend the day. We sent for Ted to make up a threesome, borrowed a kit from the professional and put in thirty-six holes at the club; and Ted insisted and I agreed that if Harrower had brought his own equipment with him, he would have been six or seven up instead of four down to Ted at the finish. Harrower said the conventional thing; but it had frequently occurred to me that when he was in form, and possessed of his personal set of clubs, he must be excellent. I asked him about it.

"Oh, I'm an in-and-outer," he said. "I have n't played since January, except a couple of rounds in California."

"You had a course out there, did n't you? What was your handicap?"

"Out there? That's hardly a criterion," said Harrower. "I'll play about a metropolitan five."

Now a golf handicap is in the nature of a Bradstreet rating, only more so. Occasionally you do hear of a composition made by a concern with first credit, but you'll never hear a five handicap man called a poor player by any one who knows that a caddy is n't a part of a teaset, and that a birdie has nothing whatsoever to do with ornithology. So, when Harrower associated himself in this fashion with the mighty, I realized that I might as well do my quota of gloating on the spot,—I had also beaten him,—because I probably should n't have

106

many opportunities in the future. And in a way, it was fortunate for my reputation that I did gloat a tiny bit; for new members of the club are inclined, these days, to regard me with pained incredulity when I say that I once had a lead of one hole over Francis Harrower in a full day's play.

In the evening after Harrower had engaged his room by the week, we called again at the Ashtons. Ted requisitioned a slice of meat for the dog, so that we had the use of the cocoanut matting, and tested out several interesting theories against a background of canvas. The stars were still shining. On the walk home, Harrower expressed profound approval of them.

" If I had n't had so many disappointments," he observed pausing, " so that I *know* I 'm almost middle-aged, I 'd feel like a youngster again — coming home from a party! I 've got myself back in the spirit, old man. It 's partly the vacation I 'm having; and partly the environment. The sky used to look exactly like this! "

" Disappointments! " I said. " What are you doing — fishing for compliments? "

Harrower grieved spontaneously.

" Do you realize that never in all my life have I got anything I started for? Why would n't that make a man feel old? "

"Forgetting college?" I reminded him.

Harrower shook his head.

"I did n't do anything at college worth lying about."

"I seem to remember," I said, "how we used to hunt for your name in the papers. If you did n't really do anything, Frank, you must have had a mighty clever press-agent."

"If I had a nickel for every time my name 's been in the papers for what I 've *done,*" said Harrower, "I 'd have a nickel. That was a three-bagger against Cornell with the bases full — but even that was n't necessary. I was a pinch-hitter in the eighth, and we had 'em six to two already. *I* did n't do anything at college."

"It seemed to me you were mighty active —"

"Oh, yes, I was. I was the perennial substitute. I was always the man slated to go in next if they needed one; and except in that Cornell game, I never got the signal. I was on the second squad in every-thing, including scholarship. I never did a darned thing in my life. Now, you take a chap like Star-buck —"

"What 's wrong with your golf? That 's satis-fied you, has n't it?"

"Runner-up cups," he deprecated. "Second

prizes. Consolations. I've got a trunkful of 'em. I'm *always* beaten in the finals. And if it's a medal play, I come in second or third — gross and net both. I never knew it to fail. I haven't a first prize to my name. And it's the same in business. If I put in a bid for a contract,— any contract, any time, anywhere,— and then if I deliberately knock all the profits off my estimate, simply to get a job and break the streak, it's an absolute certainty that I'll be the runner-up — second man! Somebody else underbids me by an eyelash; and then makes money on it! For a job in Hong Kong there were three of us — I stood second. For one in Manilla there were thirteen — I stood second. For this one in Honolulu there were thirty — I stood second!"

"Personally," I said, "if I could be sure of taking home a red ribbon every time I showed, I don't think I'd exactly hate myself."

"You would if it got to be a habit. Oh, I make *money* — but it's leavings. I was a sub-contractor on the structural end. I was asking about Starbuck —"

"What about him?"

"He's pretty popular, isn't he?"

"Yes, he's fairly well liked. Especially around the golf club. He always was."

"He was at school, I know." Harrower stopped before the Inn for a final prospect of the constellations. "They seem to think a lot of him up on the hill."

"He's rather strong there, I think. Old friend of the family, lots of money, pleasant personality and all the graces — he's a good man."

"Yes — there's no doubt about that." He hesitated momentarily. "Is there anybody else — up there?"

"Plenty of hangers-on, but nobody with any margin — not that *I* know of."

He laughed shortly, and turned to mount the steps.

"Runner-up, runner-up, runner-up!" I heard him say under his breath. "Second man *again*. Wouldn't it make you *tired?*"

Any unqualified statement to the effect that all the world loves a lover is pure balderdash. What the world loves is conflict and competition; and, after the announcement is once in the papers, public interest — except among the caterers and the bridesmaids — is recessive. What the world loves is the uncertainty of who's going to get her.

At the end of six weeks I knew Harrower as thoroughly as any man may ever know another; and I had his innermost confidence; so that I was probably the only person in Pomfret, besides the protagonists and, to some extent, Ted Ashton, who was certain of reliable information. The natural result of this contingency was that both Ted and I were periodically pumped, especially by girls who thought that their diplomacy was equal to blinding us to their purposes. We were consistent in our reactions — we had nothing to say: and the reason we had nothing to say was largely because the affair looked very much like a stalemate between Harrower and Starbuck.

Harrower was at the Inn for an indefinite term; he was commuting regularly and finding it not unpleasant; but as time went on, he began to develop symptoms of discouragement. I'm almost positive that nothing but his election to the Golf Club kept him with us after he once was convinced that Starbuck had the inside track.

"I'm going to stay on for the championship," Harrower said wearily to me, "and after that I'm going to live in town — just as I ought to have done in the first place. When a man hasn't a chance in the world to win, he ought not to clog up the field. That's *my* idea."

I hoped that my glance would anger him, but it didn't.

"Are you going to quit after one trial?"

"Trial?" he repeated. "I don't know what you're talking about. There has n't been any trial."

"You know what I mean."

"No, I don't. If you think I've said anything to *her* — well, you're mistaken, that's all."

"You have n't *spoken* to her?"

"Of course I have n't! and I'm not going to — now. I've got eyes, have n't I? And I've got fair perspicacity, have n't I? And there's no use in stirring up a mess here, and making everybody feel all the worse."

"But, my dear fellow!" I said. "I've never known a man yet who went out with the intention of losing like a gentleman who did n't do it! Why don't you go ahead and *win?*"

"A man *would* be a fool," said Harrower, "if he broke his arm on the first hole of an open tournament, and then kept gritting his teeth and saying to himself: 'Keep steady, old boy; you can break eighty! You can do it!' Now, would n't he?"

"That is n't a fair comparison. If you had ten cents' worth of confidence in yourself —"

"Confidence! Now don't get this wrong! It is n't that I'm afraid of Jimmy Starbuck, or anybody like him. There's more to it than that. Can't you see what a frightful hypocrite I'd be to suggest a — a partnership of *any* kind — with anybody? Think of the actualities! I'm a habitual failure. I simply have n't got the punch, and it's on my nerves. I have n't a good disposition to live with. I'm sore at myself. I want to *win* things. I could n't decently ask anybody to go into partnership with me in business, could I, without showing some inducement? It's the same in this case. I'm not proud of myself — I could n't expect any one else to be proud of me; and I refuse — I absolutely refuse — to involve any one else, whether it's in business or not, until I *have* done something to be proud of! Accomplished something! And not second place, either. You see, I'm looking at the future. It might be rosy for a while, but after that there'd be a devil of a lot of unhappiness, because I'm what I am. Now I'm not sulking or shirking; I'm simply saying that I'm breaking my neck trying to *do* something, and until I do I won't insult . . . You see how it is, don't you? I'm not going to consider myself eligible for — for — for Peggy, if you *will* have it — until I've made a success! My idea in going back to town was to work. And I'm going to work until I've got my nerve back, if it takes a year. Later, I'll take on all the Starbucks in the world! . . . Let's go over and shoot a game of billiards."

There are a few occasions when a man feels justified in meddling, and this was one of them. I'd
known Peggy for a good many years; and there
was n't the faintest possibility of my proving to be
a John Alden to her Priscilla. So, when the omens
were propitious, I went up to the heights, and took
half an hour to switch the conversation around to
the championship tournament.

"Ted thinks he ought to get out as far as the
finals, this year," she said. "I do hope he does; he
was bitterly disappointed last year."

"He's going very well," I conceded. "He'll
take a lot of beating."

"I'm really sorry for him," said Peggy. "He
began to do his worrying a month ago, and he's
kept it up ever since. He's got a perfectly awful
temper, and he won't eat much, and he hardly sleeps
at all. You'd think it was something really important!"

"I don't know so very many men — or women,
either," I said, "who have a good sense of propor-
tion. And nearly everybody exaggerates public
opinion. Nobody'll think any less of Ted if he
does n't even qualify. But I know a man who's
worse than Ted is — much worse. He's a good
fighter, but he has n't a great deal of luck. If he's
beaten, either in play or in business, he enjoys the

belief that he's temporarily damned by society.
I'm sorry to say that he's beaten very often. It's
Francis Harrower."

" *No!* " said Peggy blankly.

" Oh, but it is! Why, a few days ago I was talking to him about a business deal. Would you believe that he wouldn't make a partnership agreement that was unusually promising, simply because
he's fallen down on a number of contracts recently
and lost his nerve? He honestly felt that he wasn't
a good risk. Therefore, he wouldn't take the
gamble of dragging a partner into the ditch with
him."

" Why, how *funny!* " said Peggy. " He — why,
I never thought *that* about him! "

" Neither did I," I said, "until I'd known him
rather a long time. Curious how different people
are, isn't it? I can't fancy myself shrinking from
the public gaze because I was beaten in a golf
tournament — or because I'd lost a contract. But
Francis thinks he's a marked man — he won't take
any more chances."

" Chances? How do you mean? "

" Everything," I said. " He thinks he has permanent fallibility. I don't believe he'd take a
chance in a raffle for a million dollars if it only cost
him a dime — he just naturally expects to lose any-

thing he tries for. Too bad, is n't it? A man loses a lot when he won't take a chance."

She made no answer.

Harrower had promised to stay through the tournament — obviously with the faint hope of inaugurating a fresh career with a minor victory. The Saturday and Sunday before the qualifying round he spent with me in localities averaging four miles from the Ashtons. On Monday we played together.

" I 've got two possibilities this month," he said, just before we started. " This competition is one, and a contract for cement up in Dutchess County is the other. I 've shaved it down to the last sou, and if I don't get it *this* time I 'm going to jump off the Brooklyn Bridge and say: ' Here goes nothing!' Oh, don't take that too seriously — I mean, I 've got to get away with one or both of 'em — that 's all! If I don't — oh! if you only *knew* how I loathe this runner-up business!"

Whereupon he drove two hundred and sixty yards straight down the course, and the tournament was on.

The qualifying round was thirty-six holes, and the highest score to squeeze into the first division was 167. I missed it only by ten shots leeway, and

Harrower was more disappointed at my ineptitude than he was by his own defects on the seventeenth hole in the afternoon — two hooked drives out of bounds, eventually costing him seven for the short hole, and giving him a total of 147. Jimmy Starbuck, incidentally, was medallist with 145. But I was n't entirely displeased by fate, because with Harrower, Starbuck and Ted actively employed, I hoped for the opportunity to do a litle missionary work with Peggy, as we followed one of the three around the course on successive Saturdays. The difficulty, however, proved to lie in the difference of our desires; she was for trailing Ted, and I was attached to Harrower. The emergency seemed to justify war tactics, however, and I went with Peggy. It was my sole method of monopolizing her, for in the evenings she was invariably entertaining one of her squad of suitors. Besides, I wanted her, by appreciating the mental sufferings of her brother under stress, to fathom what I was hinting to her about Harrower.

Ted Ashton, who had turned in two 75's in his qualifying rounds, breezed along triumphantly all day, and won without pressure. He had taken the first hole, and never lost the lead.

"Who does he play next?" asked Peggy, when the match had become a sinecure.

"I'm sorry," I said, "but he plays Frank Har-rower — that is, if Frank wins to-day, too."

She looked at me soberly.

"He's going very strongly, is n't he?"

"He tied the record a week ago — and he's averaging down in the low seventies."

"That's too bad — no, I don't mean it's too *bad* — but Ted — you can't *imagine* how he'd set his heart on getting as far as the finals. He's sort of — desperate about it. It's been in his mind all summer long. He would n't care in the least if he lost then, but —"

"I know," I said. "And the odds are about twenty to one that he won't get past the second round. It's tough, but it's golf."

"He was awake nearly all night — I could hear him walking . . . Really, won't he give Francis a good game?"

"I'll tell you better to-night," I said, and I meant it.

Harrower had won his match at the extra hole, and he was jubilant about it.

"Luck!" he said. "Why, it was positively ludicrous! I shot like a fool, but why should n't I have some luck for once in my life? Why, once I was in the rough, and played out with a jigger, and the ball would have gone a mile past the hole if it had n't hit the flag and dropped dead! I got an eagle! And in the two rounds I holed five shots from off the green!"

"Bully!" I said. "Keep it up! But what kept your match so close?"

Harrower laughed.

"I tell you, I played like a duffer. I ought to have been licked about ten up and nine to go. But . . . Ted won, did n't he?"

"Easily."

Harrower stared at me, and at vacancy. At length he coughed, and exhaled slowly. We were, at that moment, mutually occupied in recalling Ted's tremendous ambition, and his sister's interest.

"Well," said Harrower. "If my luck holds —"

And on the following Saturday, it held doggedly. It pursued him so that it trampled on his heels and gave him a commanding lead of five holes to take to lunch with him — it was a certainty.

We ate together in silence, Harrower and I. When he lighted the one cigar he allowed himself, he looked at me with a dry smile and said: "Peggy was n't out there this morning, was she?"

"No," I said. "She was coming down to meet Ted and see the finish this afternoon."

"I wish she would n't," he said irritably. "It

won't be any circus for me to trim Ted with *her* looking on — and it certainly would n't be much fun for me to *lose*."

"Forget it!" I told him. "This is a *contest*. The man who deserves to win is the one who comes out ahead. Let 's smoke on the veranda."

At one end of the veranda was a shady niche containing a settee; and here we rested in peace. Below us on the lawn, completely hidden from us by a hedge of evergreens, was another settee; and from it a murmur of voices floated presently up to us; a man and a girl were talking; and at the same instant we realized that they were Ted Ashton and his sister.

"Never mind," Peggy was saying soothingly. "What difference does it make, anyway?"

"*Difference!*" said the boy's voice, thickly. "That 's just like a girl!"

Harrower put his hand on my arm and gestured as if to ask if we had n't better slip out of ear-shot. I pointed to his shoes — they were hobnailed.

"I 'd have given anything in the world to get to the finals of this tournament," said Ted, brokenly. "*You* don't understand! Here I 've been blatting all summer about it; everybody *expected* me to get through. It 's the only thing I 've ever really wanted. And now — to get walloped like *this*, in

the second round! He's got me —" There was
a queer, muffled sound from the lower settee; then
we heard Peggy's voice, impulsively: "Oh, don't!
Teddy, Teddy! Little brother . . . *don't!*"

It was incredible that hobnails should make so
little noise on a wooden veranda. As stealthily as
I could I followed Harrower to the nearest French
window, and together we went back into the grill.
He was sternly downcast, and there were deeply
graven lines about his mouth.

"Odd thing," I said, "that a boy as old as he is
should take it so hard."

Harrower shook his head.

"Oh, I don't know. Heaven knows *I* can't criticize him. The fellow who does n't care whether
he wins or loses does n't climb very far. And
Ted's awfully high-strung." He drummed on the
table.

"It won't do to concentrate on it," I said.
"You'd better come out and putt a few minutes.
You were getting shaky on the last couple of
holes."

"Yes, it's late," said Harrower. "It would n't
do me any harm to get the feel of the clubs, either."
Near the first tee he took my arm and spoke subdued. "She's been talking a lot about golf — and

about Ted — this last week . . . I'm wondering what was behind it?"

"You practise your putting," I ordered him. "And don't be afraid of the hole." And obediently, he went to work, and sank ten and twelve-footers with the greatest nonchalance.

It was several minutes before Ted and Peggy joined us; the boy white and joyless, the girl inspirational. She hardly noticed Harrower; she greeted him, of course, but after that she remained at her brother's elbow until the appointed hour, and when the second half of the match began she merged with the small but enthusiastic gallery, and avoided both Harrower and me. That was disconcerting.

Still more disconcerting, however, under the circumstances, was Ted's virtual collapse on the first hole. He hit a tremendous ball far off the course, made two spasmodic attempts to recover, and picked up as soon as he saw that Harrower was sure of no worse than a five. He halved the next one, holing a long approach-putt, and Peggy bravely led the applause from the gallery. Harrower took the third in a par 3 — and could have won it just as certainly with a 4. They halved the fourth, with Ted getting down his putt on the very ultimate oscillation, and Harrower annexed the fifth with a birdie 4 to Ted's 6. He was seven up with thirteen to go; and it was at about this point that I observed him glancing first at his opponent, and then at Peggy, after every shot.

The sixth was another long hole; when Harrower had driven superbly down the alley, he came over to me and said something in an undertone.

"What 's that?" I demanded.

"I 'm too far ahead," said Harrower, watching Ted Ashton founder his ball abjectedly. "I 'm too far ahead." There was in his eyes an expression which no man wrapped up in victory should have permitted to tarry there. "What bothers me is —"

"Come on, old man — talk while we 're walking."

"Oh, yes . . ." We saw Ted murder a spoon shot from the rough. "*Do* you suppose there 's such a thing as unselfishness in this world?"

"How do you mean?"

He smiled faintly at me, and nodded in the direction of the gallery.

"After all, what 's the furore about? It 's only a game . . . and there are two people crazy to have Ted get away with it, and —"

"Frank Harrower!" I said, aghast. "If you think it 'll be a fair thing or even a decent thing for you to throw this match —"

"Nobody 'll know," he insisted. "I could do it like an artist. I would n't do it for Ted, because

123

this is a fight — the better man *ought* to win. But for somebody else —"

"Frank!"

"Just to show you . . . " And with such masterly skill that even to me the essence of his imperfection was absolutely veiled, he hooked over into trouble. "There!" he said. "Who 'll question it?"

Stunned and shocked, I tugged at his sleeve.

"Frank! Look here! This is n't —"

"You let me alone," said Harrower with finality. His face was radiant, and his voice was low and steady. "And watch a man crack under the strain!"

"Frank!"

"Not if it 's evident — not if *he* suspects. Otherwise —" He blew a kiss to the clouds. "Good-by championship!" He got a half, and on the tee, Ted Ashton, laughing nervously, opined that it was all over but the shouting.

"I 'm ahead now," said Harrower, as he prepared to drive. "Still, you never can tell — I generally blow up about here —" and sent a towering skyscraper into the rough.

Eventually he won from Ted Aston at the very last hole; and he won simply because it was necessary for him to win. Admirably as he had counter-

feited wildness through the green, he couldn't
counterfeit an attack of nerves; no one would believe that a man so cheerful and composed could pass
from par golf to execrable golf without warning.
He played as badly as he dared, but he did n't dare
to resort to consecutive sixes and sevens, and nothing below those figures would have sufficed to present Ted Ashton with the match.   Not once, but
twenty times, I saw him glance first at Ted, wet and
shaken, then at Peggy shaken with her loyalty; and
deliberately ruin a shot which hardly a novice could
have missed so badly.   He labored to lose with as
pertinacious zeal as earlier he had labored to win;
he went so far as to take forty-eight strokes for the
last nine holes — par thirty-five.   But he 'd overlooked one factor in the equation.   It was physically
impossible for him to lose; he tossed away six holes,
but Ted would n't accept the seventh, and square the
match.   They were all even on the tee; and poor
Ted, so tumultuously upset that he could n't retain
a firm grip on his club, put ball after ball into the
waters of the pond.   His fourth was over; and although Harrower used a high tee and a jigger, he
carried the hazard comfortably, and on the green
found himself with four putts for the hole and
match, and a yard between the ball and the hole.   He
knew that he could n't batter the ball five times; he

knew that he could n't conceivably attain his object without detection, and he surrendered. He holed his putt; shook hands with Ted and went into the clubhouse silently. It is n't often that a martyrdom is rejected by a burlesque.

"Francis," I said to him, later in the evening, "do you know you 're a natural-born idiot?"

Harrower laughed. "How so?"

"Don't be evasive, old top. You simply are!"

Harrower looked at the floor.

"Why — the poor kid wanted it so badly: it may have meant more to him than it did to me — and I thought —"

"Oh, rubbish! You were n't thinking about *him!* You said so yourself. A golf tournament is n't an entertainment for charity!"

He reddened.

"Well, it — it got to me all of a sudden," he confessed. "I was just booming along there — I 'm not enough of a four-flusher to pretend I did n't want to win — and then all of a sudden it struck me. There was one thing I could do for her — it was n't much, but it was something. It was — oh, well, it 's all over now."

There was nothing to be gained by argument, and Harrower had n't succeeded in losing so that I did n't continue the discussion; but I could n't help wondering if Peggy had sensed his plan to discount one of the dreams of a lifetime to satisfy the vanity of a boy. I doubted it; I don't believe in what is popularly known as feminine intuition; and I thought she had been too thoroughly depressed by her brother's failure, and then too madly exhilarated by his gains, to notice Harrower's procedure. I remembered that she had n't even repeated the banal phrase of congratulation at the last hole. I resolved that sooner or later she was going to understand that unexpected slump of Harrower's; and where the motive originated. And I implored the law of chances to bring Harrower and Jimmy Starbuck together in the finals. For more reasons than one, that would be a match worth seeing.

And in due time, and by virtue of fresh conquests, they were bracketed; but long before the day of the finals Pomfret was electrified by news which, it had come a month earlier, might have caused the golf history of the county to be rewritten. Jimmy Starbuck, who had conducted a methodical, systematic campaign for nearly a year, proposed to Peggy Ashton and had his answer. On the following morning Mrs. Ashton, adopting the euphemism of "asking advice," told her best friend about it, laying down restrictive covenants of holy secrecy; and the best friend told her own second-best friend, and she told her own marriageable daughter, who was never more animated than when she was confronted by romance, and by that time the report was in everybody's mouth, and nobody was astonished.

The report was simply that Peggy and Starbuck weren't formally betrothed, but that there was an understanding.

I myself told Harrower. He was certain to hear it, anyway, and I felt that my formula might be more kindly than some others. To my intense gratification, he took it unflinchingly.

"Well, Jimmy's a good lad," he said. "It was to be expected."

"You'll play through just the same, Francis?"

"What? Play through? Of course I will!" He grinned without displaying mirth. "We'll stick to the schedule and fight it out on Saturday — I wouldn't miss it for a farm! Slim sort of revenge, isn't it? Just a minute. Was this — this thing announced, or is it just talk? Think I ought to say anything to them about it?"

"I shouldn't; it only leaked out."

"Too bad!" said Harrower. "If I'd only heard it sooner — why, I wouldn't have *thought* of beating Ted. I could have been in — in San Francisco by this time." And that was the sole evidence of his bitter disappointment and chagrin.

He had played his semi-final round excellently, with no repetition of that bewildering reversal of form which had come upon him in his match with Ted. Starbuck had also won handily, and turned in a seventy-two on his afternoon round. When the pair went to the first tee on Saturday morning, a goodly section of Pomfret was there to see — and incidentally to scrutinize Peggy, and try to analyze her behavior toward at least one of the finalists. A hundred residents of the suburb were sufficiently interested in golf to tramp behind the last survivors of the championship sixteen, and there were at least fifty who came out of social curiosity. It was a pretty gathering; I could only hope that Harrower would n't be deceived by what was purely sentimental interest in Starbuck. I did n't want him to think that because the gallery focused primarily on Starbuck, there was any implication of inherent partizanship in his behalf. But I could n't bring myself to tell him this; since the truth might have produced the same effect upon him as the misapprehension. I merely showed, as best I could, the trust I had in him.

They went at it hammer-and-tongs. Both were dashing players, scornful of conservatism, and more elated by a bold steal than by a par figure obtained by painstaking caution. Beginning on the tee, both played strictly for the hole; they disregarded the length of carries over traps and rough; they pitched for the pin, risking everything on back-spin: on the green, they ignored the sinecure of two putts, and chose the alternative of one or three. Starbuck drew first blood with a birdie on the second hole; Harrower robbed him of the third by means of a marvelous out from sand. They came to a dog-leg, and played straight over the trees instead of circling around them; Harrower's ball was unplayable; Starbuck cleared, and took another birdie.

"Wait!" said Harrower to me. And thereafter he increased the length of his already adequate swing, and hit even harder; adding ten, fifteen, twenty yards to his drive, and accepting with equanimity the occasional lies it brought him in the rough. He squared the match again, and again fell to the rear. Starbuck had entered upon a streak of miraculous putting; and went to the turn in 35, two up.

In their abandon, they were creating records in elapsed time. The gallery was forced to walk swiftly, to trot, finally to run; Starbuck was long-legged and Harrower was lithe as a panther; they teed for the water-hole an hour and forty minutes from the moment of their start. Starbuck made a two, and Harrower was three — he was four down for the morning round, and Peggy had cried out in delight at his final putt. Curiously, Ted Ashton and I alone delayed to encourage Harrower.

In order to insure his poise for the afternoon, I had arranged for us to lunch together, somewhat aloof. While he was changing his shoes in the locker-room I picked up the morning paper which I had n't seen before, and turned to the financial columns to discover how some infant securities of mine were getting along. A dozen times I was interrupted; I had scarcely unfolded the sheet when some one spoke to me; he was replaced by another; and by a third; I had n't yet inspected the quotations when Harrower emerged from the lockers, and took his seat.

" Well, what 's the news? " he asked.

" Not much," I said.

" I did n't see the paper this morning. Let 's have it, will you? "

All at once, out of a maze of type, I caught Harrower's name. I stared again, and cold chills chased down my spine. There, in a space of ten or twelve lines, was the conventional announcement of contracts let for the Dutchess County bridges and culverts. At the head of the list stood the name of a big contracting firm, with a bid of five big figures; below it, the name of Harrower, exactly a thousand dollars outbid. Out of twenty competing firms, he held his customary position — he was the runner-up! And not the subsequent item, stating that he had been awarded a trivial secondary contract amounting to six or seven thousand dollars, in which the profit must have been practically negligible, could blind me to the fact that once more he had failed. He had failed in one of the two events which were to be settled within the month; and he had come in four down to Starbuck.

"Anything interesting?" he inquired over his cold beef. "Let's have a look at it, won't you?"

"There's nothing in it — I've got to give it back. Just borrowed it for a second," I said.

"No mention of the Dutchess awards yet, is there?"

"I don't see it," I said truthfully, turning the page.

"I've a hunch that I'll land the big one," said Harrower. "For the first time in my life, I've got a hunch. I'm going to get that contract, and I'm going to beat Jimmy. Something tells me I'm going to." He grinned boyishly. "Too darned bad I couldn't have had a hunch in some other field — wasn't it?"

"You keep your mind on golf!" I commanded. "You 've got to beat par this afternoon — the way *he 's* shooting."

"Watch me!" said Harrower. And under pretense of returning the paper to its lawful owner, I went out and crumpled it into a fireplace.

He set out cool and collected, and his balance was n't the least bit disturbed when Jimmy Starbuck won the first hole by virtue of a sharp approach which landed dead to the hole, and stuck. Just as he had done in an earlier match, Harrower was glancing at his opponent and then back at Peggy after each shot; but now he was playing with the smoothness of a well-regulated machine. He had lost the first hole, but he took the next two; he halved three in a row and then won three, two of them in a stroke under par. The match was squared, with nine holes to play. And Starbuck, shorn of his advantage, had grown querulous and irritable. He muttered to himself, and displayed vast impatience. Once, when Harrower had holed a fairish putt, Jimmy had struck his club upon the ground in vexation; and I knew Jimmy's faults as well as I knew his higher qualities, and knowing them, I was restless.

The trouble began at the tenth. Jimmy was

down in five, and Harrower was playing for a half
—a matter of six feet. Overcome by his eagerness, Starbuck was dynamic. He seemed to be incapable of standing still. He fumed and fretted
and stepped about the green until a warning
" She-h-h!" went up from the gallery, and he was
checked by the sheer weight of public opinion.
Harrower was bending over the ball, careful now,
and infinitely accurate, when Starbuck exploded.

" Sink it, Frank!" he snapped.

Harrower, startled, moved his putter inadver-
tently. It touched the ball; but Harrower, presumably mindful of the penalty, had his wits about him,
and in a vain endeavor to save himself, continued
the stroke. He missed the tin by a half-inch, stood
erect, and looked at Starbuck.

I held my breath; and waited for Jimmy, who was
proximately responsible for Harrower's break, having been guilty of the flagrant breach of etiquette
which caused it, to concede the half. It was a crisis in itself, that hole. Who before had ever been
present when a finalist harried his antagonist by
speaking to him at such a time?

" One up!" said Starbuck, and turned away.

Harrower said nothing, but I saw the lines on his
face deepen. I did n't venture to look at Peggy.
The referee opened his mouth; closed it. The mat-

ter was beyond his province. And in the meantime, Starbuck had taken his stance, and was waggling in anticipation of his drive.

They halved two holes; on the thirteenth, Harrower got home on his second shot, and was again on even terms, with five to go. He looked across at Starbuck, and smiled slowly.

"Jimmy," he said — and the gallery craned to hear him —"Jimmy, I'm still wondering why one of us hasn't defaulted!"

"Your honor," said Starbuck gruffly, and Harrower laughed outright, and teed. He won the fourteenth in par, halved the fifteenth, lost the sixteenth when his iron shot found sand, and stood one up with two to play.

Never in all my life have I seen a man lose his senses so completely as Jimmy Starbuck lost them then. Considerations of courtesy, of gentility, of fundamental honesty forsook him, and left him helpless with wrath, devoid of principle. He took to standing within the range of Harrower's vision just as Harrower drew back his club to swing — and Jimmy didn't stand quite still. Twice he coughed and mumbled an apology when Francis was at the top of his swing. Once he dandled an iron, so that the light flashed back from it into Harrower's eyes. He was mad, vitriolic, berserk.

And yet, through it all, he had n't entirely squandered his prestige with the gallery; for the gallery was unobservant of detail. The episode on the tenth green passed as an accident; and Starbuck's strategy on the last few holes was totally overlooked.

Starbuck won the seventeenth; and the championship hung on the eighteenth hole.

Harrower and I were standing together at the tee and I was urging him to use the iron when Jimmy came over to us, unsmiling. His manner prepared me, in a way, for dire unpleasantness; but I was unprepared for the full vigor of his last offensive.

"Francis," said he, "if I 've got to lose this match, I 'm glad it 's to you — because I 'd hate to see you smeared twice the same day."

"I beg your pardon?" said Harrower, very stiffly.

"I said I 'd hate to have you smeared twice the same day."

"That does n't mean anything to me."

"The other deal refers to your contracts."

Harrower started. "What 's that?"

"Well, naturally, it would be some consolation if you pulled through *this* — after losing the other."

"I don't know what you 're talking about," said Harrower.

"Why, you saw the 'Record' this morning, did n't you?"

"No."

"Oh! I thought you knew —"

Harrower whirled to me. "What's he talking about? Did you see anything in the 'Record'?"

"*No!* Play your game out!"

Starbuck gestured admirably.

"Oh, I 'm sorry, old chap! It was there just the same. You came in second."

"Starbuck," I said, "if you win this championship I hope you 'll be proud of it! It's your honor. If you 'll go ahead and drive, we 'll leave the rest of the conversation for the clubhouse. Or — preferably — somewhere behind it!"

"No; let's have it out right here!" said Harrower. "You say it was in the paper — I *lost!*"

"You stood second," said Starbuck.

The referee sauntered over to us, and eyed Starbuck coldly.

"Anything I can do?" he queried. "Not talking rules, are you?"

"There are n't any in *this* match!" I said. "The only thing you can do is to make Jimmy drive; we want to get it over with."

As Starbuck went to the sand-box, Harrower touched my arm.

137

"It won't do any good to cover up *now*," he said. "I 'm braced for it. Was that in the paper? *Was I second?*"

"Francis, I 'm sorry —"

"All right; never mind." He gazed at Jimmy's screaming drive well over the pond on the line of the flag. "Not much of a man for hunches, am I?"

And after that Harrower, who had gone through more torment in a single tournament than the average man experiences in a busy season, weakened under the triple ordeal, topped to the water, took five to Jimmy's three — and it was all over.

The crowd engulfed us. Starbuck, half dazed by the shock of victory unforeseen, was swept along toward the clubhouse; the surging wave passed over us; the last stragglers hurried to be in at the presentation; we two were alone on the eighteenth green.

Harrower stooped wearily to tie his shoe. To my inexpert judgment, it did n't need tying at all.

"Well," he said, "I certainly did ruin that last hole!" And that was his solitary comment.

We went up to the house, and entered from the rear, to escape the crowd. Later we dodged through the side-door, and so to the Inn, where we dined, by special dispensation, in my room. At half past eight Harrower rose, and changed his tie for one of mine that he liked better.

"Going to make a P. P. C. call," he observed. "I'm tired of Pomfret — think I'll get out to-morrow. Don't want to come with me, do you?"

I had sufficient intelligence to decline.

"Don't sit up for me," he said. "I don't know when I'll be back. Oh! Get a copy of the 'Record' for me, will you?"

I promised; and Harrower went out into the night.

It must have been twelve o'clock when I awoke. I was sitting in a chair by the window, and on the floor was the book I had intended as a mental stimulant. Beside me was Harrower, flushed, beatific; and in his hand was a silver trophy, which he thrust upon me with incoherent ecstasy. I stifled my yawn, and took it.

"Oh! Your cup! Pretty nice for a second, isn't it?"

"Second! Why — why, I *won!* Oh, not *golf!*"

Suddenly I got it.

"Francis!" I yelled.

"I *told* you I had a hunch! I *told* you so! She knew — she knew about my match with Ted! She knew it all the time! She saw through it! She knew that, and she knew what happened to-day! Oh, she's wonderful — simply wonderful! There wasn't a word of truth in that rumor,— not a word! Jimmy *did* ask her, and she put him off — and to-day settled it! He was just leaving when I got there! Think of it, old man — a poor dub like me! I didn't lose — I *won!* You can't stop me now! I can do *anything* — anything in the world —"

"Oh, Francis!" I said. "I wish to thunder you'd landed your contracts, too! *Wouldn't* it have been a day?"

"What difference does it make?" he said rapturously. "What difference does *that* make? I tell you, a runner-up cup is pretty blamed good, if you want to know it. I'll land the big ones sometime. Give me time — I'll get 'em! I tell you, I'm just coming in for a streak of luck! Didn't I tell you so yesterday? *Didn't* I?"

THE LUCK OF THE DEVIL

FOR some mysterious reason, entirely beyond my power to analyze or to explain, I seem to be regarded by all retail salesmen as the apotheosis of Prospect. They perceive me; they instantly drop the fawning attitude which previously they have worn; and they begin a strong and merciless offensive which generally creates some real embarrassment between us before the engagement ends. They are insistent; they are relentless, and the worst of it is that I am a man of sympathy and understanding. I know that this is their livelihood, and that I have all the external aspect of an easy mark. So that I do sincerely try to buy something, if I can only find something I remotely want, because it is only by actual charitableness that we can find peace in this world and in the world to come. Often, however, it is very difficult for me to reconcile my tastes with the merchandise which is offered me.

For example, the train-boy had first dallied at my elbow with cigars, cigarettes and chewing gum; bonbons and chocolates; fresh candies; and had gone away offended, and not in the least appeased by my perfectly frank statement to him that I was suffering from indigestion. Then he returned with all the popular magazines: "Life," "Puck" and "Judge"; "Century" and "Scribner's" out to-day; and hung around me for a full minute, and departed with fresh wounds in his vitals, while I had gnawing sorrow in mine, for the poor lad was in ill health, and the train was running light. Presently, however, he appeared once more, bearing all the latest novels; new romance by Robert Chambers, out to-day; all the latest fiction; and he rested his burden on the arm of my chair and argued with me, attempting to crowd me into a corner and leave me only the alternative of buying a book for a dollar and a half or another book for a dollar thirty-five. My heart ached for him; I asked kindly if he had the current golf guide.

He said a horrid word under his breath, and fled down the aisle; but at length he came back with the paper-covered compendium in his hand, and delivered it to me. At the same moment a very stout gentleman who was sitting opposite me coughed in a terrific explosion, and, glancing up, I saw that his eyes were riveted upon the red-bound guide I had just bought. He was staring at it in what seemed very like genuine horror, and because I am by nature a student of my fellows, I became at once interested in a passenger whose emotion was so potent and so acute, and due to such an apparently trivial cause.

"Pardon me," I said. "Would you care to look it over?" I offered him the book.

His bow was courteous, but his expression was tragic.

"Thank you — *no!*"

"I beg your pardon; I thought you were looking at it."

"I was," admitted the fat man. "I was. The sight of that volume startled me. But golf ceased to have any attraction for me three years ago. I've stopped playing."

"Is it possible?"

"It is gospel truth," he said, savagely. "I have played, and I have stopped. The habit, I can assure you, is harder to break than the bonds of alcohol and tobacco. And sometimes I wish it had been harder."

"I should imagine as much. You really cared for the game, I take it?"

"*Cared* for it! Yes — once. I do yet. I love it! I loathe it! I'm through!"

"Indeed," I said. "That's most astonishing — it's unique. Every one threatens now and then never to swing a club again; I did n't realize that any one ever meant it."

"*I* meant it!" said the fat man, belligerently. "And I would n't look at that book of concentrated degeneracy for — for a hundred dollars. Oblige me by putting it out of sight. Thank. you." Uninvited, he stepped across the aisle, and seated himself in my section.

"Surely," I said, "you must have had great provocation."

"The basis of our grandeur is almost invariably the basis of our downfall," said the fat man, permitting his features to relax dolefully. "And a golf tournament is like a pool of contaminated water: it corrupts itself and everything else in the neighborhood."

"My chief pleasure in the game," I hastened to assure him, "is intellectual. My handicap is fourteen; but as an experimental chemist of the links I'm behind scratch."

He eyed me steadily.

"My reasons for quitting the game were n't technical; they were sentimental." In response I ventured to display a curiosity which was utterly sincere, and quite spontaneous. "Very well," he said, breathing stertorously and gazing at me stonily, "if you *will* have it.

THE LUCK OF THE DEVIL

"When you come right down to the determining
factors in any man's success or failure, you can't
eliminate luck. I *defy* you to eliminate it! Take
the Duke of Wellington. Where would be his place
in history if Napoleon had ordered a different
menu? Or, if you follow the other theory, if
Grouchy had n't been deaf; or if his guide had n't
been stupid. Take Newton, and suppose his apple
had n't fallen until the next day. Take Watt if his
mother had n't made him watch the kettle. Take
Columbus if a bit of driftwood had n't floated
along. What would have been the result? A Con-
tinental empire, a country schoolteacher, a village
blacksmith, and a murder on the high seas. Pur-
sue the analogy. Take anybody you choose; I 'm
going to pick a superlative and call him Brown. I
knew him well; I 'll tell you about him.

"This Brown was incredibly lucky. He did n't
have luck in streaks; he had it always. He could
have set down luck as one of his tangible assets and
borrowed money on it. If the regular phrase to
indicate fortune is to say that the baby was born
with a silver spoon in the mouth, then this man
Brown was born chewing a whole tea-service of flat
silver in dozen lots. And if he 'd had the added
luck to be born deaf, dumb, and blind, he 'd have
been a millionaire before he was old enough to vote.

That sounds funny; I mean that he 'd have done better if his luck had n't been complicated by his intelligence. Now and then, you see, he relied on his judgment; when he did, he got stung. As a matter of fact, he 's a millionaire now, but it 's taken him thirty-four years because he was n't wise enough to discount what little honest mental capacity he had and put all his hope of glory into the hands of Providence.

"And then, on the other hand, take another chap named Smith. He was unlucky. He was as extreme as Brown was; he was simply a butt for the world to haw-haw at. These two grew up as boys together. When they went skating Brown fell through the ice, and Smith went after him to pull him out. Smith got pneumonia, and Brown got a medal for life-saving. If they went to steal apples, Smith got caught and whipped, and Brown got away with all the fruit. When an old pupil came back to the school and offered a prize of ten dollars for the best speller, that was the only day in six months that Brown knew his lesson, and he corraled the ten dollars because Smith had got the whooping-cough the day before.

"That was the way it went in college, too. If they had an examination, all the questions were from exactly those few parts of the course that

Brown had crammed last night, and Smith had skipped not so much because he was letter-perfect in them, but because they did n't seem to him to have permanent value. The last place on the base-ball team was between the two; while the coaches were deciding in favor of Smith, he was busy over in the gymnasium doing setting-up exercises to strengthen his muscles, and falling downstairs and breaking his arm. Brown, in the meantime, was playing poker. But that afternoon, with the bases full and two out, Brown ducked to get out of the way of a wild pitch; the ball hit his bat, rolled fair, and won the game. So Smith was a substitute for four years, and never got his letter; and people said Brown was a genius because he 'd sized up the situation, and bunted when the fielders naturally expected he 'd bang it out.

" Those are merely incidents, but they 're indications. After the two were graduated, they continued the same old procedure. They bought the same speculative stock at the same figure. There was a panic; some securities went both ways at the same time. This stuff of theirs dropped eleven points; Smith telephoned his brokers to sell at the market; he 'd swallow the loss. Brown *tried* to telephone, but the line was out of order. When he got down-town in a street-car, the stock had recovered twelve and a half ·points. Think it over.

"I could quote a thousand examples, but I won't. My illustrations are typical. Understand, however, that the two men were inseparable. They were the closest of friends. Smith never envied Brown — never. He took his medicine with a smile, and gloried in his friend's triumphs. He never allowed himself to be pitied. And Brown invariably refused to capitalize Smith's misfortunes, although, in the light of later years, it is questionable if this was forbearance or simple negligence. Never mind; for many seasons their friendship was rarely beautiful until — you have probably guessed it — they fell in love with the same girl."

The fat man paused, and raised his eyebrows significantly. The club-car attendant was hovering nearby.

"Thank you; a glass of seltzer," I said.

"And for me," he told the attendant, "a glass of French vichy, with the juice of a quarter of a lemon in a separate glass, and one small lump of ice in a saucer, and a spoon. Bring a full bottle of vichy, and uncork it here; and if the ice is n't absolutely clear, I 'll send it back. To resume:

"Yes, in the course of time they fell hopelessly in love with the same girl. None of your knitting, tatting, pink, and peachlike beautiful dolls, with an ingénue stare and a lapful of Pomeranians and fondant creams; not a bit of it! She was a dashing, smashing beauty, a big, healthy, athletic girl full of vim, vigor, and vitality. She read the newspapers; she talked politics like a man; she was fit to be an executive and a disciplinarian. She could sit a horse like a bronco-buster; but she believed that women are downtrodden and oppressed. The equality of marriage was one of her principles. Obviously, she was n't popular among old-fashioned young men: but Smith and Brown were bowled over simultaneously; they saw what a life-partner that girl would be. They adored her, and they were n't ashamed to talk about it. That, if you please, is the highest compliment a man can ever pay to a woman.

"Make no mistake; they were still friends — friends when Smith must have appreciated the almost insuperable obstacles placed in his path by the luck of Brown; friends when Brown must have been sorely troubled to acknowledge as an intimate a man who made so many egregious blunders as Smith. Yet I insist that from the very beginning the girl was not averse to Smith.

"Brown? Oh, *he* was always lucky. We won't waste time with *Brown*.

"Presently, of course, each asked her to marry him. To each she gave the same answer: sisterly affection and more; she could n't decide between them; time alone would tell. And *still* they were friends.

"But eventually there is an end to all things. That, I think, is an axiom. And no matter what may be the foundation of friendship between two men, no matter what hardships it may have overcome, no matter how solid and substantial it may seem to be, it cannot withstand the gentlest of all the elements.

"At length Brown said to Smith: 'My dear fellow, things have gone crossways with us. Why prolong the agony further?'

"And Smith said to Brown: 'For twenty years, ever since you got a medal because I tried to rescue you, and I got pneumonia for being rescued, you 've come out ahead in every contest. This time I 'm going to win!'

"And Brown: 'But suppose that instead of staying on in this way, watching our friendship beat itself to pieces on the rocks, and politely knifing each other, so that a third party might come alone and cut us both out — suppose that we settle the difficulty neatly and promptly. One withdraws; the other has a clear field. Let 's make sure that *one* of us is successful.'

" Smith was no fool; he knew that if luck were to swing the balance anyway, he was already beaten.

" ' What 's your suggestion? ' he asked.

" ' I 'm so fond of you, dear boy,' said Brown, ' that upon my word I 'll be almost as happy if you win as I should be if I won myself. I 'll leave it to hazard. I 'll toss you to see which of us stays here, and which of us leaves within ten days for a trip around the world at the expense of the other. Out of sight, out of mind. And if the one who stays home is n't engaged or married by the time the traveler comes back, then he 's to default and give the traveler a clear field.'

" ' Hardly! ' said Smith.

" ' Well, have *you* anything to suggest? '

" ' Golf,' said Smith. ' Eighteen holes match play — with a referee.'

" ' It 's a bargain,' said Brown. ' Personally, I think it 's a bit unfair, but it 's a bargain. You know very well that the best I ever made was a seventy-nine, and I average about ninety to your seventy-eight.'

" ' That does n't signify,' said Smith. ' You never cracked eighty more than once because you did n't need to. You win every handicap tournament you ever enter, and you usually win it by a

margin of one stroke. This is different. Your natural luck is coming into action. I'll hedge. I'll
bet you a thousand dollars you're eighty or better
in our match.'

"'It's a bet,' said Brown. 'To-morrow at one-
thirty?'

"'I'm content. Who'll referee?'

"'Bert Jones?'

"'It's a bargain,' said Smith. 'But, mind you,
we're going to stick to the rules.'

"'Also the conditions,' said Brown. 'The loser
sails within ten days, to be gone not less than ten
months. And that'll quite clear the situation, because she's admitted that if either one of us had
never met her, she'd certainly be married to the
other by this time. One-thirty?'

"'On the dot,' said Smith.

"Now there's no reason for you to be prejudiced
against Smith because he selected golf as the test
when the apparent superiority of his game over
Brown's was so great. To be sure, Brown had
broken eighty only once, but he was a marvelous
match player. He was steady as a church, and if he
got an eight on one hole, he got a three on the next.
Smith played in the seventies but if he went off his
game, he was liable to be in the nineties. At
medal-play Smith would have had a tremendous

edge in his favor; at match-play the odds were even. I am telling you this to avoid misunderstanding.

" To resume. At half-past one on the following day Smith and Brown, with Jones, the referee, were on time to the minute. Miss Robinson was also there; somehow the story leaked out. Possibly fifty other members of the club were also there. The contest was romantic; it suggested the age of chivalry, and a battle in the lists for the lady's hand. It caught the public. Smith and Brown, who had expected a quiet little struggle to the death, found themselves in the presence of a pretty fair gallery. They did n't like it; but what could they do? It was too late; their contract was in force, and neither would relent. The referee tossed a coin; Brown won the honor. He drove."

The fat man regarded me soberly.

" For very good grounds," he said, " I can recall every stroke of that match. If you are bored, say so. I should dislike to bore you."

" Pray proceed," I begged him.

" With pleasure. To resume. Brown drove. As usual from the first tee, he sliced. A bunker was correctly placed for the specific purpose of catching a sliced drive from that tee. It was a high bunker, with rough grass on it. Furthermore, the face of it was soft from a recent rain. Brown hit it on the fly.

"'Tough luck!' said Smith, who was by far the better sportsman of the two.

"Smith drove perhaps two hundred and fifty yards straight down the course, and the gallery applauded; but Smith ignored them. It was his customary drive. He was one of the best drivers in that vicinity.

"The gallery set itself in motion; on arriving at the bunker Brown began to hunt for his ball.

"'Over here,' said his caddy, pointing.

"Brown turned, incredulous. The ball was out on the fairway.

"'How did it get there?' he demanded angrily. 'You didn't lift it, did you?'

"'No, sir. It hit a rock and bounced back.'

"The gallery spread out in a long V, and Brown hit a good mid-iron shot somewhere near the green.

"'Where's mine?' asked Smith.

"'You're in the brook,' said the referee, Jones.

"It was a fact; Smith's magnificent drive had rolled into the water, which was intended to penalize a poor second shot. It had never happened before; it hasn't happened since. That two-hundred-and-fifty-yard screamer had crawled another hundred yards over the smooth baked turf.

"'One up,' said Brown, going to the second tee as soon as Smith had broken his niblick on the small stones of the brook.

"The second hole was about two furlongs; Brown topped into the tall grass, opened his mouth to discuss the shot, remembered Miss Robinson in the gallery, and let the profanity ooze through his pores. Smith sent out another superb drive, and counted the hole as won. Unfortunately, nothing but skill and courage were on his side; Brown had the luck. Brown attacked that tall grass with a brassey, something that Lee Maxwell himself would n't have done, and got enormous distance — something else that Lee Maxwell would n't have done, because I tell you plainly, it was n't humanly possible. But Brown did it. He was still away; he played an approaching cleek, ran into a sand trap, hopped out to the green, and was dead in three.

"'Great work!' said Smith, without sarcasm.

"He himself played dead to the hole: a long shot, exquisitely accurate. Brown went down in four. Smith addressed the ball with a putter.

"'You touched it!' said Brown. Every one looked toward the referee.

"'Did it move?' inquired Jones.

"'It did,' said Brown.

"'I yield to the judgment of the referee,' said

Smith, and he waited composedly for the verdict. He was unshakeable in his poise.

" 'I think it moved,' declared Jones. 'It costs one stroke.' Whereupon Smith also holed in four . . . three actual strokes, and one for the penalty.

" 'Still one up,' said Brown, grinning idiotically. 'Now all I 've got to do is to halve sixteen more holes, and the match is mine.' He swung easily as he spoke. The hole was a short one; but his iron was wild, and the ball swerved sharply to the left, flying towards a horrible plot of stumps and geology. If he got in among the obstacles, he was doomed.

" 'Oh, hard luck! hard luck!' said Smith.

" 'Wait a second!' snapped Brown. His ball had ricochetted amazingly from the trunk of an oak-tree. He was not only safe; he was on the edge of the green; he had a sure three. 'Beat that if you can!'

" 'I 'll do my best,' conceded Smith, modestly, and with never a thought of the breathless crowd behind him, he drove in perfect form. He could n't have placed the ball more neatly if he 'd done it from two feet away instead of from two hundred yards. It was a club's length from the cup. Brown came up and got his three, and took off his cap to acknowledge the applause of some of his friends.

Smith had taken his stance; Brown's cap hit him on the shoulder, and with innate consideration Smith moved aside.

"'Pardon me, old fellow,' he said, courteously.

"A gasp and then a roar went up from the gallery; Smith had accidentally stepped on his ball, and crushed it into the turf.

"'I'm sorry, Smith,' said the referee. 'Rule Twelve — costs you a stroke.'

"'Does it?' Miss Robinson was coming forward. She had no jurisdiction, but she had what served her as well — a sense of justice. 'That is n't fair!'

"'These gentlemen are playing golf according to the rules,' explained Jones. 'Smith has a chance for the half.' Miss Robinson attempted to protest, but he waved her off, and Smith holed for the half. That was the second opportunity he had missed because of technicalities.

"At this juncture the gallery was pretty evenly divided. Public sentiment generally operates in favor of a good loser, but public sentiment always inclines toward a good fellow who has a little luck. It was about half and half. The merits of the case were still in abeyance.

"Once more Brown drove poorly, and once more Smith cracked out a shot with the low trajectory of a bullet. Nevertheless, both were on in three. Brown putted, and then Smith putted — too soon. He had an eye like an eagle, and the delicacy of an embroiderer; the ball traveled straight for the cup.

" ' My hole ! ' said Brown, gaily.

" ' How 's that ? '

" ' My ball had n't stopped moving.'

" Smith looked blankly at the referee. You may judge of his emotions, for this was his third disaster on consecutive holes. 'Is that a fact ? '

" The referee nodded sorrowfully.

" ' But I distinctly *saw* it stop,' said Smith, not in the way of a protest, but rather as a minority report.

" ' It virtually stopped,' said Jones, ' but the wind must have taken it, and it moved ahead again. It surely was oscillating when you played. You lose the hole, and Brown 's two up.'

" It was noticeable that Miss Robinson had left her place among the spectators, and ranged alongside the referee. She was rather agitated; she wanted to argue about the nobility of judicial decisions. But the referee was adamant.

" ' Now then ! ' cried Brown, waving his driver. ' Fore ! ' There was no one in front of him; the warning was for the evident purpose of attracting attention, although the man who 's driving has usually more attention than he likes. Not so with Brown. Furthermore, his drive was n't remarkable for anything but its height. As for altitude, it was prodigious. Oh, yes, it was straight, too — for the first time that day. But Smith outdistanced him by twenty rods. That 's conservative.

"'Over the ditch from here!' bragged Brown, selecting a heavy brassey.

"'Look here, old fellow,' said Smith, 'that is n't golf! That 's suicide. You can't carry it from here. Don't be reckless. Play safe for a half. You 're throwing it away.'

"'Keep your eye on Uncle Cyrus!' said Brown as he slugged away in execrable form. The ball scurried along the ground like a frightened mink. It was hit hard; it had steam behind it. It headed squarely for a motor-mower. 'Fore!' yelled Brown, this time in deadly earnest. The chauffeur of the mower, paralyzed with fright, hesitated and finally dodged. The ball struck a projecting boss of metal and leaped skyward. It landed on the half-hidden cover of a drain, and bounced again. When it came to earth it was over the ditch. Never before in his life had Brown got so much distance with a brassey; it was superhuman. The players halved in a par five.

"'I do hope,' remarked Smith, going to the tee,

'that we don't need any more referee's decisions. I'd rather like to finish this match without prejudice.' He played a full mashie, and on my word of honor, he holed out! Down in one! It's only a hundred and forty yards; it had been done before. You seem pained; wait a moment!

" 'After *I've* driven,' said Brown, coolly, 'you can take that shot over again.'

" 'What?' Smith was staggered; no wonder.

" 'It was my honor,' said Brown. 'I have the privilege of recalling that shot. I do recall it. You were out of turn.'

" 'Bert,' said Miss Robinson to the referee, 'is that right? Can he do that?'

" 'The rules state —'

" 'I don't care *what* they state; that was a wonderful shot. Are you going to take it away from him?'

" 'I'm afraid I am,' admitted Jones. 'I'm here to interpret the rules of golf. It's mighty tough; but Brown had the honor, and he's entitled to it. By virtue of the authority vested in me I direct Brown to drive, and Smith to drive after him in his proper turn.'

" There could be only one outcome: Smith's nerve was shaken. Brown was none too clever from the tee, but Smith was worse. He lost by a stroke, and stood three down. Figure it for yourself: morally he was five or six under par and three or four up; actually, however, he was three down. It seemed inconsistent.

" The seventh hole was normally a drive and an iron; there was a stone wall running parallel to the line of flight, and a row of shaggy trees running along with the wall. Brown hooked viciously into the trees. Ninety-nine times out of a hundred that would have been out of bounds; but no! the ball rattled around among the limbs, dropped to the top of the wall, and leaped nimbly out to the fair green, where it ambled peacefully up to a tuft of grass and sat down. The gallery cheered delightedly; even Miss Robinson had to applaud. Nobody paid any special heed to Smith, who was stinging another clean shot down the alley; a lot of people can hit straight balls! Why, when the crowd found that Brown was all teed for his iron shot, they cheered him again, just as though some merit accrued to him for being lucky! And nobody thought to groan because Smith was squarely behind a mole-cast!

" No, not even when Smith played a masterly cut shot to the edge of the green did he get the sympathy of the gallery; for Brown, banging away, caromed off the stone wall again and was on the edge of the green! Both played well up in three; Brown holed in four, and Smith was sure of a half — the putt was n't over two feet.

"Now, a good many matches are won and lost within two feet of the hole. Vardon has lost some, and Braid and Chick Evans and John Anderson have; but mighty few golfers ever missed a putt as short as that for the same reason that poor Smith missed it. He hit a grasshopper.

"Long before this, Miss Robinson had begun to share with the players the absorption of the crowd. Regardless of appearances, she trudged along with the referee. She seemed to find plenty of amusement in Brown's luck and some source of regret in Smith's, but as for open leaning toward one or the other, there was n't a sign. When Brown sclaffed into the pit on the eighth, her expression altered not the slightest; and when he played out with a nickel-plated lofter, her face was slightly flushed, but still inscrutable. She showed no more emotion on discovering that the ball had landed in a shallow trench just short of the green and bounded comfortably close to the pin than she did on perceiving that Smith's excellent approach had overrun by a yard or two and gone down a small shaft where there had once been an irrigating-pipe.

"'My hole!' said Brown, with rather more joy

than the circumstances warranted. 'Your ball's unplayable.'

"'I think not,' said Smith, deferentially. 'I think I can drop a club's-length away without penalty.'

"'Mr. Referee?' said Brown, with a rising inflection.

"Miss Robinson sidled nearer to Mr. Jones, and looked at him narrowly. Her lips moved as though she were getting ready to say something.

"'I am of the opinion,' he declared, 'that Smith loses the hole. It's a rub of the green.'

"'But if the pipe had been there,' said Miss Robinson, unable to restrain herself, 'and his ball was unplayably close to it, he could have lifted, and dropped without penalty, could n't he?'

"'He could,' said Jones.

"'So he loses the hole simply because somebody took that pipe out of the ground this morning?'

"'He does,' said Jones.

"'But that is n't golf!'

"'It's in the rules,' said Jones, 'and Smith is five down. So far he has n't made one mistake, and Brown has n't made one good shot. You 're right; it is n't golf; but it 's the official score.'

"'For my sake,' said Miss Robinson, so that several bystanders overheard her —'for *my* sake, won't you be lenient enough with these silly rules so that there 'll be some sort of *contest?* This is only a farce."

" The referee straightened himself manfully.

" ' The links is no place for leniency,' he maintained. ' I 'm here by special request of both parties to administrate according to the rules of the game as approved by the Royal and Ancient Golf Club of St. Andrews, and as adopted, with amendments, by the United States Golf Association, of which this club is an active member in good standing. Regardless of the private questions involved, I find that if a ball lodge in a hole recently vacated by a water-pipe, and is unplayable therefrom, the player loses the hole. If the water-pipe had been there, Smith could have moved away from it. It 's Brown's honor.'

" So that Brown, having the gratifying lead of five up, drove lustily for the ninth. His was a high drive into the wind; it was unmistakably ticketed for the sand-pits. The ball reached the zenith of flight; it began to drop, and at that moment an unexpected gust of wind came whistling over the hills, and Brown, instead of being in the sand where he belonged, was ten yards short of the pits, on good turf. Smith drove handsomely; a ball apparently destined to clear the hazard with something to spare.

Another gust of wind, and Smith was nicely bunkered.

"Outlucked, but never outgamed, he chipped prettily out, and ran down a long putt for a three. Brown took four. It was the first hole he had lost; even so, the match was in his pocket."

The fat man looked covertly at me to see how I was taking it.

"It's a pretty fair story," I said, "but one day down at Pinehurst where I was playing with Roy Durstine, he —"

"Brown is four up with nine to go," he reproved me. "To resume. It would be far beyond my power as a truthful man to relate, or yours as an experienced golfer to believe, that Brown was equally fortunate on all of the eighteen holes. I hope I haven't given you that impression, because it's unjustified by the facts. On the tenth, for example, he reverted to his regular game. He foundered his ball off the tee, missed his second shot completely, went into a cop bunker and out again, and took four long brassies to the green, where he went down in three putts. At the eleventh, which was ridiculously short, he sliced into a roadway, foozled again, but drove a good-sized pebble a hundred and seventy-six yards straight down the course; was on in six, and down in seven. At the twelfth he foozled, topped into grass, went out in three, into the pond in four, out in five, on in six, down in eight. That made him dormie six.

"I repeat, that made him dormie six. Two of those holes he won and the other he halved. Let me detail Smith's progress for those same holes. At the tenth, when Brown was five and Smith was two, Smith lost his ball. After that, when Brown was four and Smith had driven ever so slightly into the rough, his caddy, hunting for the ball, kicked it down a woodchuck's burrow. The twelfth they halved. It was like this:

"Brown, as I said, took eight. Smith made two hundred and forty yards off the tee, and was on the green in two. Miss Robinson's bull-terrier, which had joined the gallery recently, picked up the ball in his mouth, and started for the clubhouse with it. I claim that it was wholly natural and spontaneous for Smith to run after that dog, and feint at it with a putter. I shall always insist that there was sufficient aggravation for Smith to hit the dog with the putter. Of course it was injudicious of Smith, considering who owned the dog, to punish the animal for mere playfulness; but it was worse than injudicious for him to hit it with the putter, when he could just as easily have kicked it. After a moment or two of skirmishing, the terrier retrieved the ball, and deposited it on the green. Smith, not daring to glance toward Miss Robinson, holed out, and said, ' Three.'

" ' Not three — eight,' said the referee.

" ' That 's what *I* made it,' agreed Brown, winking at a friend.

" ' I — don't understand,' faltered Smith. ' If a ball at rest is displaced by any agency outside the match except wind, the player shall drop a ball as near as possible to the place where it lay without penalty.'

" ' *You* did n't drop it; the dog dropped it,' said Brown.

" ' Yes, but he dropped it within an inch of where it was originally.'

" ' Let the referee decide!' said Miss Robinson, softly, and every one turned to Jones.

" ' This is n't a case of law,' he judged, after some deliberation; ' it 's a case in equity. If the ball had lodged in anything moving, Smith could certainly have replaced without penalty. He 'd be down in three. Of course the ball did n't *lodge* in anything moving, but it was immediately taken up *by* something moving, and found lodgment therein. Smith could have recovered the ball and played it; but he did n't. Furthermore, he did n't strike the dog with a stick or with his foot; he struck it with a putter.

167

He did this with the apparent intention of causing the dog to drop the ball nearer the hole. I adjudge that this act of Smith's operates as a waiver under rule Seventeen. I adjudge that Smith's strokes with a putter at the body of the dog count as fair strokes. He had five of them. If he had n't made them, and the dog had carried the ball away, or even refused to give it up, I should have declared it a rub of the green; and directed Smith to drop without penalty. His official count for the hole is therefore eight. Every attempt to compel the dog to disgorge, inasmuch as the ball was struck at, and not spooned or pushed, was a stroke. The hole is halved, and Brown is dormie.'

"I will not deceive you; the gallery was dazed and bewildered. In dead silence Brown drove off, a futile attempt which barely cleared the tee-box. In all that gathering, the only person whose mental processes were working placidly was undoubtedly Smith. He carried the green with a beautifully placed iron; and neither the fact that he had knocked the ball into a prolate spheroid, nor the ill fortune he had to find it lying between serrated ridges pushed up by worms, could deprive him of a par three and the hole.

" He won the fourteenth with a par four, and the fifteenth with a par five. The luck had apparently turned, and the sentiment of the gallery was changing also. The applause was all for Smith, and Miss Robinson's smiles, too, were frequently directed at him. He was as calm and unconcerned as though the match were for nothing more important than the caddy fees; Brown, on the contrary, was noticeably afflicted with nerves.

"And the sixteenth hole was no place at all for a man with nerves. Directly before the tee a swamp full of weeds and muddy lagoons yawned hungrily for a topped drive. To the left, there was a deserted quarry; to the right, a corn-field. Nothing but a hundred-and-sixty-yard carry uphill, nothing but a perfectly straight ball, would do, and Smith topped into the swamp. So did Brown.

"The gallery stood about on dry land and watched intently; the two contestants, followed by Jones and Miss Robinson and her dog, picked their way into the wilderness. Smith's ball was found first; it was resting conveniently in a small puddle, under a couple of bullrushes, behind a jagged rock.

"'Shoot from there,' said Brown, cheerfully.

"'I intend to,' said Smith.

"'What are you waiting for?'

"'For you to find yours,' said Smith.

"'Why, mine's right around here somewhere. Go ahead!'

"'Not yet. If you found yours farther from the hole than this is, you'd take advantage of the rule about the more distant competitor playing first, and recall the shot if it happened to be good, and let it go if it happened to be bad. I want to see where yours is.'

"Brown looked at the swamp. He was standing on a board, and he had previously observed that Smith, while he was talking, had settled in rich mud up to his knees, and was still sinking.

"'Shoot!' said Brown. 'If you get out of there, I'll promise not to recall your shot.'

"'I stand on my rights,' said Smith. 'My ball is here, and yours isn't in sight. It may be lost. It probably is. If you don't find it inside of five minutes, it's my hole.'

"'But if you get out in one shot,' said Brown, 'I'll *give* you the hole. Don't you see? If you get out safely, there's no reason for me to ruin *my* clothes!'"

"'How's the time, Mr. Referee?' asked Smith.

"'One minute left.'

"Brown stepped gracefully from the board. The leg he put forward disappeared utterly; the other clung to its harbor; Brown looked a good deal like those photographs of the diving horses at Coney Island. To the accompaniment of huzzas from the

"If you get out safely, there's no reason for me to ruin *my* clothes!"

crowd and much encouragement from Miss Robinson, he struggled free, and staggered, and brought up sharply with a cry of dismay. He had trod on his ball, and driven it clear under the surface of the mud.

" ' Two! ' said Smith, with a shade of genuine feeling for a discomfited enemy. ' Remember, you can displace only so much of the mud as to enable you to see the ball.'

" ' I know,' barked Brown. ' Niblick, boy! '

" He dug for that ball with all his strength; it popped lazily in the air with a reverse English, avoided Smith's mud-puddle by the fraction of an inch, and came to rest on the very board from which Brown had stepped into the swamp. It could n't roll, because of the clayey mass adhering to it. It presented a very decent lie for the next shot.

" Brown looked wickedly at his opponent and then at Miss Robinson. He failed to catch her eye, because she was looking somewhere else; but the roar of the gallery encouraged him, and swiping with his nickel-plated lofter, he carried the slope of the green.

" ' *Now* shoot! ' he called cheerily to Smith.

" Smith did his best; it was n't good enough: the ball imbedded itself still farther in the mire. He struck once more; his club came over his left shoulder at the finish of a fine swing, but the ball did n't soar away as it should. Indeed, it had simply disappeared. It had n't risen from the swamp; it was n't on the fairway; it was n't in the puddle.

" ' Dig for it,' said Smith to his caddy, and at that moment a terrific shout went up from the circling multitude.

" ' Now 's your chance, Smithy ! '

" ' Be careful ! be careful ! '

" ' Turn your club over — *quick !* '

" Smith, puzzled, inspected the face of the club. The grip almost slipped out of his hand; he caught it by a convulsive effort. The ball, almost entirely enveloped in black, sticky mud, was firmly attached to the roughened metal.

" ' What — what do I do with *this?* ' he inquired blankly.

" ' Drop it without penalty,' said Brown, too hurriedly.

" ' Is there anything in the rules to prevent me from carrying this up to the green, and dropping it in the hole? '

" ' If there is n't,' said Brown, ' there 's nothing to prevent any one from jostling you while you 're on the way.'

" ' I think I 'll try it,' said Smith. ' I 've read somewhere of it 's being done. It was a very funny story. I remember I laughed a long time about it.'

" ' If you do, it 's my hole. That was a ball at rest displaced by an agency outside the match.'

" ' Not in a thousand years! This club of mine has been in the match since we started; so have I.'

" ' It is n't good golf,' said Brown, paling.

" ' Never mind. It is n't luck, either. More than that,' said Smith, eyeing Brown coldly, ' if you jostle me, that 'll constitute an infringement of my rights to play my own game. You 'll be deliberately disturbing the lie of my ball. I leave it to the referee.'

" ' Smith is right,' pronounced Jones. ' I can't think of any rule to cover the point, so we 'll decide it in accordance with common law. The ball must be played from where it lies. Smith played it from there. It now lies on the face of his mashie. His next shot must be played with a different club OFF the mashie. *De minimis non curat lex.* Nevertheless, there is some precedent for assuming that the stroke made by Smith is yet unfinished. The face of the club hit the ball. That 's obvious. It was a legitimate hit. Now, everybody knows that in every shot the face of the club is in contact with the ball for a more or less appreciable space of time. The stroke is consummated after the ball has left the face of the club. This ball has n't left it at all. The stroke is therefore still in process. So we have two theories, one that Smith's ball is now at rest, in a lie from which the next stroke must be played; the other, that it has n't come to rest after the stroke he *did* play. So that if he goes to the green and with some other club knocks the ball off the mashie into the cup, he will have taken three strokes, which gives him the hole in three. If we adopt the other theory, and he merely shakes the ball into the hole without using a separate club for the purpose, he will have holed in two, which again gives him the hole. In either case he wins. Brown will be dormie two. Finish the hole, Smith, and it 's your honor.'

"The crowd laughed and cheered. Brown stalked wrathfully across the footbridge to the fairway, picked up his ball, and threw it at his caddy. The referee instantly awarded the hole to Smith. Miss Robinson, taking the referee's arm, called him a Daniel come to judgment. He was all of that.

"Smith won the seventeenth in four. Brown needed eleven. It is only fair to state that Brown had fallen into his old weakness; instead of playing by sheer guesswork, he was calculating his shots carefully, and trying to gage the wind and estimate the speed of the greens. While he held to that method he had n't a chance in the world; and either he realized it himself or some one reminded him of it, for when he took the tee at the last hole, he merely waggled his driver once or twice, made no endeavor to stand properly or to swing in form, and as an obvious consequence — obvious to those who knew his attributes — he got off his very best drive of the day. It was n't more than fifty or sixty yards behind Smith's. They played good seconds, and came to the flag on even terms.

"I won't detain you. Smith got his par five. Brown needed only a half for the match, one up. If he 'd shut his eyes and putted, there would n't have been a chance in a million for poor Smith. But Brown wanted to be a hero; he wanted to look like Walter Travis sinking a hard putt. So he studied the line carefully, and played gingerly — and missed! The match was all square! They had to go to an extra hole!

" They were walking back to the first tee for the play off when Miss Robinson and Jones joined them. Miss Robinson was authoritative — even for her.

" 'Listen,' she said. 'Don't you two men think you 've carried this wretched travesty far enough?'

" 'How?' asked Brown.

" 'I 've carried it nineteen holes anyway,' said Smith.

"'Had it occurred to you that *I* might not be willing to stand by the result of it?'

"She was right; they had n't thought of it.

"'We simply agreed,' began Brown; but she stopped him with one of her peremptory gestures.

"'Golf is a game of character,' she said. 'You 've shown me more than you think you 've shown. Go on and play your extra hole, settle your match once and forever, but bear this in mind while you 're playing it: the race is n't always to the swift — nor to the lucky. He laughs best who sees the point of the joke. Your winner *may* be the loser, and the loser might be the winner, after all. I don't say that he surely will be; but he *might* be. I only want you to remember that I have n't consented to accept your compromise. That 's all.'

"The men stared stupidly at each other. They could n't comprehend it.

"'Anyway,' said Brown, suddenly, 'I have n't broken eighty. I was much more than that. I 've won your thousand, old fellow.'

"'Yes,' admitted Smith, 'and it 'll just about pay the tips on your long trip.' But just then he began to wonder if Miss Robinson, who was notably independent, would deliberately side with the loser of the match. He glanced at Brown. Brown was palpably wondering, too. But Brown was thinking more in the past than in the future. Had he been really wise? It now concerned him to know if his rigid insistence upon the letter of the rules had hurt his cause with Miss Robinson while it was helping him with his contest. He did n't know whether to copper his bet, or not. His distress was so great that he usurped the honor, which did n't belong to him, and drove off; very creditably, too. His mind was occupied; it was characteristic luck.

"'Now, then,' said a voice from the gallery. 'Recall *that* drive, Smithy! He did it to you once.'

"'I 'll let it stand,' said Smith, loudly, as he advanced to the tee. 'This is a gentleman's game.' He addressed the ball with a flourish; by mischance he toppled it off the tee, and it rolled thirty feet downhill.

"'Playing two,' said the referee. 'Re-tee it, and drive again.'

"'I refuse to accept that penalty,' denied Brown, peering about to see if Miss Robinson was within earshot. 'Take it over, old man.'

"'Never!' said Smith. 'I play from where it lies.' He played very poorly. '*That 's* two.'

"'You have a right to decline my waiver,' said Brown, stiffly, 'but *I* have a right to adjust the matter as a gentleman should.' Here he bent over his own ball, lifted it an inch or two above the ground, and dropped it. 'I have touched a ball in play not for identification, and the penalty is one stroke. We lie alike.'

" 'I waive,' said Smith.

" 'You can't!' said Brown. 'It can't be done. Ask the referee.'

" 'The referee states,' said Jones, rather faintly, 'that a penalty may not be declined. Proceed.'

" 'Very well,' said Smith. 'I have my own ideas of sportsmanship!' He intentionally drove out of bounds. 'Drop another ball, caddy! Now I'm three, and you're two.'

" 'Observe this!' said Brown, taking his stance. 'In the act of addressing this ball, I cause it to move. That costs me a stroke. We lie alike again.' They glared at each other like two strange bulldogs.

" Miss Robinson was plainly heard to say, 'Imbeciles!'

" 'The amusing part of it is,' remarked Smith, conciliating, 'that *I*'m trying to play a gentleman's game.'

" 'You've missed it by a mile,' said Brown.

" 'I'm tired of your methods,' said Smith. 'I'll lay you a hundred I beat you this hole now!'

" 'Double it!'

" 'Make it a thousand if you like.'

" ' Certainly ! '

" ' Please play, then. You 're away.'

" Accordingly, Brown played an iron. It was too strong. It should have gone past the green, over the fairway of the seventh; but Brown was wild with anger: he did n't concentrate on the ball, and luck was with him. He hit the very tip of the flag-stick. The ball dropped dead to the hole.

" ' Four! ' he gloated. ' *Now* show something.'

" Smith turned to the gallery.

" ' Ladies and gentlemen,' he said, ' this is a match for big stakes. You 've seen that the rules have been strictly followed. So far I have n't had to rely upon bickering and trivial points; I am now about to rely upon them. I am now about to make use of a stratagem I got from the immortal works of Van Tassel Sutphen. If the player's ball strike the opponent, his caddy, or his clubs, the opponent shall lose the hole.' Smith took a heavy approaching-cleek from his bag, and looked resolutely at Brown, who winced. ' The opponent,' repeated Smith, easing his wrists, ' shall lose the hole. Sutphen got away with it, and if he did, *I* can.'

" Brown, whose knickerbockers suddenly seemed too large for him, looked desperately for his caddy; but the caddy also knew the rule; he was hiding behind the bunker, and he had pulled the bag of clubs after him. Brown glared helplessly around; and Smith kept altering his stance so as to keep him covered. He was as keen as a trap-shooter at unknown angles. Brown was only twenty yards away; he threw a despairing glance at the bunker, and caught sight of the caddy beckoning frantically. He started to walk towards this refuge; and Smith started to swing. As long as he could endure the strain, Brown strode with a remnant of dignity; he wanted to appear too proud for flight. But finally his nerves snapped; he dug his spikes into the turf and dashed for the protection of the bunker.

"Smith, who had n't been daunted at the knowledge that his opponent was dormie six; Smith, who had played the generous game from the start; Smith, who was the injured party throughout; Smith sighted for the fleeing man. And then Brown, deluded by imagination into thinking that he had heard the sound of impact, threw himself headlong, and scrambled in a panic for safety. With a fiendish laugh, Smith got the range, and drove.

"It was a phenomenally timed shot, a low, straight ball barely above the grass-tops. It hit Brown on the fore-shoulder just as he was crawling into the trench behind the bunker, and he yelled with pain, and rage, and collapsed into the sand. It was epochal.

" ' Sutphen was right,' remarked Smith, yawning casually.

" The gallery rushed forward; as the leaders passed the referee they heard him saying, ' Hole and match to Smith.' It was all over.

" The rest shall be brief. They took Brown to the clubhouse and massaged his shoulder. The two men, refined in the fire, met once more as friend and friend. They embraced. Their better instincts returned. Their bitter enmity was forgotten. They canceled their bets. At length they set out to hunt for Miss Robinson: to apologize to her, and to ask her to make her choice as she willed, but soon enough to save the fragments of a torn friendship.

" She was n't to be found. Her warning had been more pregnant than they had imagined. While Smith and Brown were risking their lives, their fortunes, and their sacred honor, she had motored back to town with the referee Jones, leaving behind her a note to say that she could n't respect a man as perennially unlucky as Smith, nor yet as culpably sharp as Brown.

" I ask you to consider their emotions at the discovery, and at the thoughts it engendered! Consider the tension they had undergone! Not only money was involved, not only default of courtship;

they had all but shattered the precious vessel of integrity! And for what? For whom? They had made of themselves laughing-stocks forever; they had gained for themselves the reputation of poor sportsmen, and worse. Even now the executive committee was holding a special meeting in the grill-room; its announcement that both Smith and Brown were expelled for excessive and unwarranted gambling on the links followed by only five minutes the shock that came from the knowledge that she who had inspired them to do this thing now scorned them both. And think what might have been! If Brown had been less sharp, he might have won a bride, even though he lost the match. And if Smith had been less buffeted by fortune, he might have had a wife to console him. As it was, the very competition which was to insure to one of them the possession of a beautiful and talented girl lost her to both forever. Within the month, she married Jones.

"That 's all."

"And lived happily ever after?" I queried.

At the nearer door an Ethiopian swayed rhythmically as he intoned the call to lunch. My fat neighbor rose precipitately.

"Not so you could notice it!" he said. "But

that's the reason I never play golf any more. That's why the mere thought of it curdles my blood. That match was the most depressing, the most terrible single episode in my whole life — and if I could blot it out of my memory by any conceivable sacrifice, I should do it, and thank my stars for the blessed privilege."

"And no wonder!" I said. "You're the man you call 'Smith,' of course, are n't you?"

He looked at me in a tumultuous passion, and yet in his eye I seemed to detect a pathos which was heart-rending.

"Oh, no," he said. "Oh, no, indeed; I would thank Heaven if I had been. Or I would give all I own to be Brown. Unfortunately, sir, I was the referee. I'm Jones."

THE LAST ROUND

OVERNIGHT, an insolent wind had dashed down in a guerrilla raid from the north, plundered the unsuspecting country as it might, and fled, frost-laden, from the sturdy counter-attack of the October sun; so that by noon the atmosphere was calm again, and unharassed. But as marauding parties, even when repulsed, leave signs of things accomplished, and plain warnings of more raids to come, so had the first of this year's gales left in the air an ultimatum, half portent, and half reminiscence; and, in the meantime, set the world a-tingle with strong light and stronger color, and the fresh stimulant of its own rare ether. The sky was none of your blued-steel firmaments, belligerent and cold; it was immaculately blue, immeasurably distant, but nowise chill, and prophetic, rather than intimidating. The sun, ever so slightly fagged from its defensive sortie, was in supreme command, yet not despotic in its domination. The temperature was that of a perverted June. And so by axiom, all sound-minded men who were unhampered by the stress of trade were out-of-doors; and those whose wisdom was impeccable were playing golf; and from this latter class a happy muster of privileged enthusiasts were taking profit from their membership at Templeton.

On the veranda of the clubhouse, three men were sitting to overlook the private driveway, and the turn-around. There was an elderly man in conventionally striking checks and wool; there was a middle-aged man in knickerbockers and Norfolk four years worn; there was a slender youth in creamy flannels. Characteristically, as they sat and watched, they smoked,— the boy a cigarette, the shabby man a pipe, the senior of the group a plump cigar. Smoking at ease, they also smoked in reticence; now and then they craned in unison at a motor gliding along the avenue of trees; occasionally they ennobled experts on the adjoining thirteenth green by rising from their chairs to estimate the difficulty of a putt, and to evolve the odds against success. At the minimum, they had maintained this lethargy for a quarter hour; they seemed as callous to the opportunity for golf, as insensible to the superb links at hand, as though they were so many uninstructed aliens, ignorant of the history of Scotland, immune to the insidious temptations bred at Templeton.

At length, the boy in flannels tossed away his cigarette, and spoke at random.

"Well," he remarked lugubriously, "it's about time, isn't it?"

The man in shabby knickers nodded patiently.

"It's late," he said, with an accent so delicate, so all but imperceptible, that few would have supposed his grandfather had gone about in kilts.

"Oh, not very," commented the elderly gentleman. "He had to get his massage, you know."

The flanneled youth scratched a match on his heel, and lighted another cigarette, taking excessive care with all mechanics of the act.

"Feels like a funeral, doesn't it?" he shuddered. "Br-r-r-r!"

"That depends on your discreemination," conceded the pipe-smoker, who had registered on the handicap list as Peters, D. A. . . . 7. "How about you, Kingsland?"

Kingsland contemplated the wrapper of his cigar, and smiled grimly. Grimness was typical of him; impertinent members referred to him as "the old war-horse."

"To tell the truth," he said, "I'm not relishing the prospect of this afternoon very much, and I don't imagine you are, either. But we've got to make it as pleasant for Norton as we can. Put yourselves in his place. . . ."

The youth, who was popularly called Bunker because his sur-name was Hazzard, had depths in his eyes as he gazed out over the landscape. He was a rhapsodist, afraid of detection.

"I wonder," he mused. "What d' you suppose *he's* thinking?"

"If you're that inqueesitive," said Peters abruptly, "go be a convict."

Hazzard sniffed. "That's hardly a parallel." Nevertheless, he slumped into his chair and considered it.

"It is n't too remote," said Kingsland, fondling his tie. "Billy Norton loves golf the way some people love life. He's been at it for twenty-two years — picked it up when it was a joke, and everybody wore red coats and thought thirty-five cents was an outrageous price for Silvertowns. Why, Billy Norton was a topnotcher when rubber-cored balls came in; he was winning sectional tournaments when young Hazzard there was going to bed in daylight. He's a student and an arbiter and a savant and an encyclopedia. I've seen him swinging on a jute mat in his garage in February, and I 've seen sixteen mashies in his house at one time. It took him a calendar year to pick the one he could trust. And —"

"Any duffer could do that," growled Peters, resting on his elbows. "But Billy Norton 's the most inveterate enemy bogy ever had. He has n't won as many competitions as some people, but for re-liabeelity —"

" The thing about him that gets *me,*" said Hazzard, "is his disposition. My Lord! When he beats you, he makes you feel he was doing his best to win, but he 's so darned sorry it had to be *you* he beat — and if you 'd been on your game you 'd have slaughtered him. And of course I have n't known him very long, but no matter what happened, I never heard him make a single excuse —"

" That 's plausible — because he never made one," said Kingsland, conveying reproof. " He told me at least ten years ago that the most valuable lesson he ever learned was that nobody but himself was interested in Billy Norton's game. . . . *How* he 'll miss it!"

Peters coughed gruffly.

" Are his doctors too meteeculous, Kingsland?"

" Hardly. There were three of 'em in consultation. You see, he was standing up in the vestibule when the crash came, and he was thrown squarely against the brake-wheel —"

" Oh, those commuters are fools," said Hazzard bitterly. " They start to pile out when the train 's half a mile from Grand Central. I thought Norton had more sense. But one bump should n't have put him out of business — he must have had a bad heart anyway."

" He did," agreed Kingsland. " But it would n't have stopped his golf unless he 'd had that terrific fall. . . . The doctors know what they 're doing."

" And after twenty years," said Peters reflectively, " they tell him that this is the last round he can ever play. It 'll be grievous hard for Billy."

There was a moment devoted, by each of the three, to altruistic revery. Alike, they were inordinately fond of the game, but not with Norton's sovereign and enduring passion. They were performers of equal distinction, but none of them could approximate, on the season's average, within two strokes of Norton. Besides that, Hazzard was the local tennis champion, and Peters a fancy skater and a famous swimmer, and Kingsland notably adroit with firearms. Norton was a golfer and always a golfer, and exclusively a golfer. Divorce him from the links, and his biography thenceforward must inevitably be a record of blank despondency, with never a chance to prove again that once he, too, had earned his pinnacle. His friends knew this, and they were sorely burdened by the certainty.

" I heard," said Hazzard, subdued, " that before he could persuade 'em to let him play this one round he had to have daily treatments for six weeks. And he had to beg like a pirate at that!"

"I hope to Heaven he can score," said Kingsland, shaking his head. "It's a wonderful day. The greens ought to be fast as lightning."

Peters shrugged his shoulders.

"After resting since the middle of July? He'll be lucky to break 90. I suggest we have the tee-plates moved up to the limit."

"Billy wouldn't approve of that," doubted Kingsland, "but if he doesn't break 80, he'll break his heart, and that's gospel. . . . He wants to finish with a good round. . . . Don't you forget, we've got to keep him cheered up. That's what we're here for." He peered fixedly down the avenue of trees, and got to his feet. "There's Billy's car now! Come on over and meet him, everybody!"

Leisurely they crossed the veranda towards the motor entrance. Kingsland and Peters were admirably composed, but Hazzard, whose temperament made him a marvelous medal but an erratic match player, was unutterably downcast. Somehow he had managed to incorporate himself into Norton's shoes, and into Norton's psychology, and his sympathies were rapidly getting the better of him when Peters, cannily alert, put out a brawny hand and gripped his unflexed biceps in a clutch which brought agony to Hazzard's face, and in a flash dispelled his vapors.

"Ouch! What in thunder 's the matter with you . . . !"

"Smile, Bunker!" said Peters, indicating the slowing motor. "This is Billy Norton's exodus from golf. Make it cheerful. Smile, damn you, — smile!" His own jaw tightened, and then his lips curved artificially. "You, *Billy!*" cried Peters with solemn boisterousness, as he went ahead.

At forty-five, Norton was a man of no remarkable physique; indeed, he would have passed unnoticed for his bulk in almost any gathering of athletes. A closer scrutiny, however, would show that muscularly he was compact and well-equipped; he was slim-waisted, but his torso illustrated the precise symmetry, with relationship to the rest of him, which trainers look for in the football squads. His hands were small, and his fingers tapering, but his wrists were bundles of tempered and twisted wire. His eyes were large, and humorous, and steady; his complexion was a tribute to his manners and customs; his entire countenance was indicative of frankness and generosity, and a certain ingrained idealism; and yet there were lines about his expressive mouth, and a solid bit of sculpturing in the region of his chin, which betrayed no lack of the attributes which men call fighting qualities. To-day these lines were cut more prominently than usual; and there was a constant contraction and expansion of Norton's pupils. A series of infinitesimal furrows had crept upon his forehead, and his nostrils appeared to be abnormally sensitive. On the veranda and in the locker-room, he had laughed easily and chatted without restraint; but from the instant he stepped out upon the sod, preoccupation had seized and silenced him. At the first tee, he had paused in introspective woe; presently he looked up, and flinched at the broadside of triple commiseration.

"Come, come!" said Norton, assuming a tone of raillery. "What is this,—a wake?"

"Er . . . I'm sorry, Billy," said Kingsland in haste. "All the good caddies had gone out. We've got four infants. Do you mind?"

Norton inspected the undersized specimen of vitality which was in charge of his clubs. The caddy was ridiculously small, impossibly dirty, but electrically alert and eager; and Norton's approbation was spontaneous. The caddy's physiognomy relieved him, too, of some of his depression.

"Not a bit," he denied. "But what I was going

to say was that I asked you three to play with me because you're the best golfing friends I ever had. So I hope you'll understand me. . . . Please don't let's bet on the match . . . just for once."

"Quite so, quite so," assented Peters. "And shall we play foursomes or independently?"

"Why, unless you . . . why don't we go independently? No teams, and no gambling. I'd rather appreciate it. Would it spoil your game?"

"No, indeed," said Kingsland with great heartiness. "We'll learn how much we're really good for. . . . You take the honor, Billy."

Accordingly, Norton requisitioned a pinch of sand from the tee-box.

"A lot of people joke me about it," he said, "but for years and years I've kept a golf diary. . . . Altogether, I've played nearly three thousand rounds of golf. That's a lot, isn't it? I've played Templeton over four hundred times. And it's . . . it's a trifle disconcerting to look off down this hill . . . and realize that if I made a bad start now I can't come back to-morrow, and . . ." He stopped, and when he resumed, his tone was deprecatory. "I hate to hold you fellows up, but I've simply got to take a couple of practice swings."

"Go ahead," said Hazzard, squinting at the

ground. "Nobody behind us." He was staggered to discern that even in so great extremities, Norton disdained an alibi.

Kingsland and Peters, side by side, were regarding Norton with evident concern. There was no use whatsoever in belittling his recent shock and illness; his quondam smoothness and adroit coordination of impulses had deserted him, and his form was ominously atypical. Even in his preliminary motions he revealed the injunctions laid upon him by his nostalgia; and Kingsland and Peters, simultaneously aware of what mishap the afternoon might bring to Billy Norton, were no less conscious of the dream he cherished, and the struggle he was making to reëstablish what self-reliance he had lost. Witnessing his faultiness, they sickened with the apprehension of pure logic.

"That'll do," said Norton, and addressed his ball.

Blindfold, any of the trio could have sensed from the sound of contact that Norton had topped his first drive. There was no precision in his swing; there was no audacity; worst of all, there was no trace of that indescribable contempt for the ball, of its antecedents and consequents, which is an integral and a vital factor in any shot. Hazzard, who hadn't lifted his head until the echo of the impact, almost groaned.   The others, unable to predict whether Norton would be more wounded by condolences, or disheartened by the lack of them, murmured incoherently.   Norton stepped back from the plates, and swished his driver at a leaf of sorrel.

"Good medicine," he said calmly, "for an inflamed conceit.   I pressed."

Nevertheless, as he later strolled down the fairway on the trail of his inefficiency, he couldn't refrain from picturing to himself the prodigious swipes he had sometime made from that initial tee. He was glad that Peters and Kingsland had got off so well — and eventually they would get off even better; he regretted that Hazzard had hooked his tremendous liner into the rough — but there remained to Hazzard a calendar full of days on which to redeem himself.   It was only Billy Norton whose franchise was running out, and couldn't be renewed. He smiled paternally at his caddy, and possessed himself of a beloved iron.

"Oh, well," he said aloud, "there's one good thing about it — we'll never make another bad start as long as we live!"

The caddy grinned, disclosing wide gaps in upper and lower teeth.

"Nope," he conceded amicably.   "We topped it, didn't we?"

"We'll make it up on this one," promised Norton.

"Huh! Betcha!" The caddy was supercilious towards failure.

Norton, warmed by the stubborn loyalty, played the iron. He had completed a cursory audit of his bodily resources; he was convinced that if he relentlessly cleansed his mind of its inhibitions, he should mechanically revert to form. He was in no corporeal pain; he was merely sluggish, and soft. And because, out of his plenteous store of golf psychology, he knew how best to grapple for the elusive item of confidence, he played the iron with all his strength; and to his ineffable satisfaction, the recovery would have done credit to Edward Ray. The trajectory was low, and the momentum great; the ball, dipping to earth after a sheer carry of two hundred yards, sped straight as a plumb-line through twin traps, and scurried on in search of shorter grass to rest in.

"Huh! Betcha!" cackled the caddy, appropriating an interest in the laurels.

Peters and Kingsland were also in the neighborhood of the green, and Hazzard, who had been nervously treading turf, and kneading it with the sole of his brassey, beamed to the utmost, and shafted his second shot without resentment. And soon thereafter, the three friends halted motionless in a little knot, and focused upon the bowed back of Billy Norton with such profound intensity that two week-end guests at Templeton, who beheld the tableau from the nearby seventh, spoke cynically of the evils of heavy gambling, which makes men importune the fates to bring confusion to a vigorous opponent. The week-end guests, however, did n't observe that when the careful player pitched within a club's-length of the cup, his three companions applauded energetically; nor did they overhear a caddy whispering loudly to his fellows: " Betcha little kernick we sink it!"

In the proper order, Norton sank it solidly, and as the ball rattled against the shining zinc, he was for the moment transported with delight which could n't be concealed. The infection burned in his veins; the sweetness of redemption soothed his soul; he was mad to hasten to the second tee, to do this thing again, again, and ceaselessly; and then, summarily minded of his status in the universe of golf, he hesitated, and his smile faded, and the lines crept out once more upon his forehead. Let the pendulum of the years wag on; let golfers come and golfers go, and stroke by stroke the incalculable sum of all the strokes increase; but insofar as the first of the eighteen holes at Templeton was included in that division of his ephemeral experience, he had achieved the ultimate. And fighter as he had always been, fighter as still he was, Norton knew that his wrists were trembling, and that the shame of senility had come upon him.

The sincere compliments of his friends rang crude to Norton; he was sentient of the forced gaiety in their tones. A wave of mortification drenched him; he wished that he had n't ventured so absurd a farewell to sportsmanship. And then, involuntarily, he smiled. He was thinking of his cyclonic feat with the iron and of the placid assurance of the freckled caddy.

"I believe," said Norton, "it 's still my honor."

There was a pronounced improvement in the timing of his subsequent swing. His normal rhythm had come home to him, and he was conciliated and emboldened by the surety of one par hole already on his card. And yet, although he battled doggedly against the concept, he was unable to free himself as soon as he had executed the shot, from the premonition that after this, each effort was certain to hurt him — to hurt him physically, locally, acutely, so that he could n't continue to play; so that he could n't consummate the round. The instructions of his physicians were piling themselves into a tumbled heap in his brain; he could recall verbatim how the medicos had argued with him when he first pleaded for the boon of this anti-climax to his career, and how they had implied that the effects of it might convert him to the belief that even physicians sometimes know what they 're talking about. To be sure, he had driven lustily and without discomfort; thus far, he had been visited by not the faintest symptom of distress; nevertheless, he was intermittently worried by what he interpreted as an intuition, and his uneasiness was so patent that Kingsland rallied instantly to his support.

"If we speed up a little," said Kingsland casually, "we ought to be able to get in twenty-seven holes. That 'll please you, won't it? The extra nine is velvet."

Norton gestured to signify the negative.

"No — a round of golf is eighteen holes. I 'd rather concentrate."

"*That 's* discreemination!" said Peters. "I 'm counting on you to hang up an 85, Billy."

"*Eighty-five!*" spluttered Norton. "Why, if I can't do a seventy-nine or better I *ought* to resign! Eighty-five! Class B stuff!"

Hazzard edged over to him, and got his attention.

"Say," he said, half-apologetically. "You 've got such wonderful direction, Mr. Norton — if you just keep on the line and don't bother about distance you can break eighty *easy*. . . . I noticed you 're hitting awfully hard."

Norton was grateful for the misplaced kindness.

" There may be something in that, Bunker, but I want to be in the seventies. I 've got to be radical."

" Here 's an example on this shot," entreated Hazzard. " You 've got a good lie; don't try to make the plateau; play safe. You 're sure of your five if you do."

Norton wavered.

" No," he declared finally. " This dog-leg is n't an accident; it 's engineering. We 're supposed to shoot for the pin. I like to go for the hole. If I flub, I *deserve* the punishment. If I don't . . . well, any novice can play short."

" It 's a deeficult carry," frowned Peters. " I 'd use the wood."

Norton deliberately chose his favorite iron.

" Boys," he said, delaying, " you 're all talking and acting as though I 'm a doddering old cripple. . . . If I 'd thought you 'd let me get on your nerves like that, I 'd have gone around alone — I honestly would! You forget it! *I* 'm not squealing. Let 's play golf!" And with the paralysis of fear exerting its baneful influence upon his poise, he topped dismally into the luxuriant weeds of remorse.

At that juncture, nothing more salutary could have befallen him. His will, grown flaccid during his weary confinement, had hitherto balked him and he had allowed himself to succumb to his own pathology, but automatically, when he saw the ball disappearing among the weeds, his reason, trained to eliminate the non-essentials, busied itself with the sole problem of extrication. His spirits rose prodigiously; and Norton himself did n't realize that he was fundamentally happier not because he had man-handled a shot, but because he had stopped thinking about everything but golf. He had utterly dissociated himself from his ailments and his gnawing afflictions; the topic of mashie-niblicks held a monopoly upon his rational faculties. As he followed his buoyant caddy through the lush vegetation, he whistled a melancholy strain which was melancholy only because Norton's atrocious whistling was chronic; it had no reference to the state of his infelicity.

"There!" said Kingsland obliquely to Peters. "If he keeps up chirruping like that, he'll shoot golf!"

And Norton was keeping it up most dolefully, in spite of the fact that his stance was uneven, and that in order to get down to the ball, he must necessarily carve through a thick buffer of rank vegetation.

He was absorbed in the building up of a working theory, and his whistling increased in volume as he pondered.

"Betcha!" announced his caddy, intolerant of the pinch. Norton chuckled, and having settled with himself the type of endeavor most suited to the lie, and to the complications of the rough, procrastinated no longer. He bent his knees a little so as to retain all possible weight on the ground, and to provide sufficient resistance to counteract a potential loss of balance; he gripped the mashie-niblick more firmly; he went for the ball with the conclusive ounce of his vigor and intrepidity. The blade tore through the slippery weeds; the ball rose sharply, cleared the intervening herbage, and fell so closely to its predetermined location that Norton could hardly have bettered his strategy if, instead of using the mashie-niblick, he had simply walked on for half a furlong and placed the ball where he wanted it.

"Great work!" shouted Peters, waving his congratulations.

"Bully!" said Hazzard, breathing deeply.

"Right on your game, Billy," acknowledged Kingsland. "But you'll have to go some for your par five."

"*I* told you so," muttered the earthy caddy.

But Norton knew that second green too well. It was an undulating green, close-clipped and perilously fast; it was hard to reach and hold, even with back-spin; and yonder there was a tract of rock and gorse, inimical to scoring and to temper. He was content to run up modestly with a jigger, and to take his allotted two putts, and a six, rather than apply for the lesser figure, and perhaps be called to judgment for an over-approach. And the consciousness that he was only one over par for two holes, and not yet beaten by his deficiencies, tended to inspire him.

The third was a matter of two hundred yards, and the quartet assailed it with renewed vivacity. It was a perfect specimen of a one-shot hole; its green was totally surrounded by sand and knee-high scrub; and in front, a serrated ridge of stubble estopped the players from any but high and accurately directed drives. Invariably it had baffled Norton; it was his bugaboo; he disliked the distance, and habitually overplayed, or, if he gaged the yardage to a nicety, rolled to a crescent trap which was the southern boundary of the green. He was inconceivably anxious now to sever his acquaintance with this hole on his own terms. He was so anxious that in his zeal to escape the fateful crescent, he put an arching shot squarely in the center of the opposite pit.

"There!" he said, explosively. "Thank Heaven it's done with! This ratty little hole has kept me awake more nights. . . . Never again!"

"A brave hypocrisy, man!" said Peters to Kingsland.

And, for a verity, Norton had prevaricated in gross. His malfeasance was a source of anguish which not for thousands would he have consented to express. Here was a sin of commission for which he never could atone by practise, or by postnate virtue. He might indeed retrieve the squandered stroke by superlative genius on some other hole, but this, the third, had ensnared him according to its wont, and so must read the docket. But he chipped out cleverly, and gained an acceptable four; and none of his comrades guessed the blackness of his vast self-condemnation.

Out of the precious eighteen holes vouchsafed to him, three were already in the past, and thirteen strokes were entered on the books. Norton, whose technical horizon was commonly defined by the very next shot, and nothing ulterior, found himself involved in simple mathematics — thirteen from seventy-nine leaves sixty-six. Sixty-six strokes for

fifteen holes remained to him; in former days the
allowance would have offered speculative possibilities. But Norton, subconsciously induced by
Hazzard's pleading, was vacillating between reck-
lessness and caution; he was obsessed by the knowledge that since he himself had set his own objective, a degeneration from it would permanently dis-
qualify him in his own esteem. Should it be rash-
ness, or conservatism? At the outset, he was inclined to yield to Hazzard.

"And yet . . ." said Norton, unwittingly aloud.

"What 's that?" asked Kingsland.

Norton started, and smiled feebly.

"I was just thinking about an old golf verse,"
he said. "It 's like this —

> "If the pleasure in golf lies in hitting the ball,
>   And in seven a hole you do,
> Then I, who have played fourteen in all
>   Have had twice as much fun as you!"

"Good stuff," said Kingsland appreciatively.

Norton shook himself, and stated profanely to his
alter ego that there must be no repetition of this
mental cowardice. It was n't fair to himself, and
it was n't fair to his friends. He had no right to
cover them with the pall of his own gloom. He
ought to plot his campaign for himself, and adhere
to it. He plotted it forthwith; and he adhered to

it so steadfastly that his application to the game was quite incompatible with social intercourse. The next six holes he played as in a trance.

Now because his friends recognized — to the extent that it is possible for one man to fathom the emotions of another — the importance to Norton of this personally inflicted ordeal; and because they coincided perfectly in a diagnosis of his wishes, they unanimously, from the moment of Norton's severance or oral communication, held their peace. They argued that he had withdrawn by choice into the solitude of his own reflections, and that tact required of them the courtesy of silence. From tee to green, and from green to tee they accompanied him; they were monosyllabic among themselves; they perceived that Norton was living in a world apart, and that in meeting and surmounting obstacles, or being blessed with and receiving luck, he was playing solely by instinct, dazedly, subjectively. He was so overwhelmed by the cruel rule which was to govern his golfless future that realities no longer impressed themselves upon him. Hypnotized by his very tenacity of purpose, he went six holes without awakening to etiquette, or to dynamics or to topography.

Still plunged in his fit of abstraction, he had holed a long putt on the ninth, and straightened himself to stare with stolid eyes at a prospect of maple trees and a reach of terraced lawn, when Kingsland touched his arm, and spoke to him. Norton jumped.

"What? What's that?" he stammered.

"You turned in forty," repeated Kingsland. "Nice work."

"*Turned?* I — why — what was that you said?"

"In forty," reiterated Kingsland.

Norton, stupefied, fell back a pace or two.

"Good God!" he faltered, rubbing his forehead. "Have we . . . *we can't have played nine holes!* I did n't . . . realize that!"

No one laughed. On the contrary, Hazzard, blinking rapidly, also took up the study of that panorama of maples, and apostrophized them in the curtest of sentences. Kingsland and Peters both coughed uneasily, and interchanged glances of smarting helplessness. They had comprehended Norton's intellectual aloofness, but they were stunned by the revelation that he had dreamed and conjured himself around in a medal forty, while supinely obeying reflexes, and gathering neither pain nor pleasure from the strange performance. And now that Norton was summoned to the material world again, he was in an agony of embarrassment; his friends no less.

In the meantime, the warmth was slowly receding from the sun, and a fretful wind was whipping across the plains. Kingsland shivered.

"Let's get started," he exhorted bruskly. "It's blowing up colder. Billy, if you don't look out, you'll lose your amateur standing! Just out of the hospital, and forty strokes to here!"

Norton smiled at him without mirth.

"Old man," he demurred, "you know I'm not complaining . . . but you certainly did upset me. I . . . I feel as though a word's been lopped off my vocabulary. . . ."

"What word's that, Billy?"

"'Turn,'" said Norton. "In the sense *you* meant it." He bit his lip and flushed; then, stiffening, he walked in a direct line to Kingsland, and faced him sternly. "Look here," he said. "If I pull any more stuff like that from now on — *brain* me! I'm making a damned fool and a baby out of myself! I haven't the grit of any oyster! All of you — I beg your pardon."

"Nonsense!" said Peters. "And keep your head down!"

"We're with you, Billy," said Kingsland.

"Same here," added Hazzard, incapable of sustained speech.

"No — I do beg your pardon," insisted Norton. "I won't pretend this is n't a hard day for me, but I don't need to be a wet-blanket *all* the time. From here on we'll have some fun out of it. My honor?"

"Right," said Peters. "Well earned."

As Norton prepared to drive, Hazzard sidled towards Kingsland, and accosted him in an under-tone.

"I thought," he said, with traces of sarcasm, "your idea was for us to keep him cheered up!"

"Well, it was!"

"And a sweet mess we've made of it, have n't we?"

"A misunderstanding, Bunker — nothing more."

"Granted — but why don't we *do* something?"

"We will. Go ahead and be facetious. He's getting a grip on himself. . . . *Nice one*, Billy!"

Norton was admittedly proud of that drive. It was the best he had yet obtained, and eventually it proved to be the best of the four, outstripping Hazzard's mighty slash by a clear twenty yards. And as soon as the party quitted the tee, it was evident that Norton was forcing himself to joviality in order to quiet his conscience, and propitiate his friends. He chattered volubly; laughed when there was little to laugh at; and conducted himself generally in a way to discount his primary ethics of a golf match. If his taciturn period had brought sorrow to the three who partnered him, this interlude of superficial glee brought with it a measure of discomfort which was irresistibly demoralizing. Hazzard's equilibrium was the first to lapse; he missed his second shot most execrably, took five to reach the harbor of the green, and went from bad to worse on the tantalizing eleventh. Kingsland capitulated on the twelfth, and picked up shamelessly when he was playing seven. Peters, steadiest of the trio, blew up at the tricky thirteenth, putting four successive spoon shots out of bounds. And through this cataclysm of bathos, regardless of the poor examples set for him, Norton went indefatigably forward, talking in little bursts of almost hysterical intensity, laughing with metallic dissimulation at things not humorous, and playing without a flaw. Negligent on the tee, he was appallingly true to the direction flag; through the fairway he was insouciant to the point of apathy; he putted without apparent discretion, and still the putts went down. For five holes he continued this wild revelry of shattered nerves; on the fifteenth he sliced to a patch of woodland, and, declining assistance, pursued his caddy in search of the hiding ball.

"Whew!" said Kingsland, when Norton was out of range. "Is n't it *terrible?*"

"Awful — awful!" Hazzard was agitated as with the palsy.

"The man 's raving with it," said Peters compassionately. "Once I saw the psychopathic ward on Sunday morning. . . ."

Within the copse, Norton and the caddy were hunting diligently for the missing ball. By this time, the wind had doubled in velocity; Norton, removing his cap, took it with gratitude, for despite the lowered temperature, his head was moist with perspiration. And as he tramped through the crackling underbush, he was unexpectedly visited by an exquisite thrill of desolation; a despairing wrench at his heart-strings which left him palpitant and numb. He could remember how often he had cursed inwardly at such contingencies as this; how he had appraised the loss of a ball as an unforgivable misdemeanor, chargeable first to himself, who had driven it off the course, and secondly to the boy who labored in vain to find it. Now he was sensing the innate sweetness of ill fortune as well as godsend; he was convinced, at the end, that golf is even greater than its own philosophy. Norton wondered what would have become of his character if he had taken other disasters as stormily as he was taking his discharge from golf. He wondered how, if his reactions to-day were congenital, he should accept more serious burdens — such as the discharge from mortality. He stood stock-still, and applied the searchlight of reason to his inbeing.

"I — I guess it 's a lost ball," ventured the caddy, surrendering to the obvious.

"Did n't you mark it?"

"No, sir — did n't *see* it."

Norton transfixed that caddy, and the boy wilted.

"That 's very unusual. Most boys say they marked it. Why did n't you?"

The caddy dug his toes into the soft loam.

"Did n't *see* it."

"I know — but most boys say they did, anyway, when they lose a ball. They don't want to be scolded, so they say they marked it. Why did n't you say so?"

The caddy reddened under the grime, and posed heron-like on one foot.

"Dunno," he answered.

"I do," said Norton kindly. "You 're all right, caddy! I 'm not going to scold you."

The boy eyed him shrewdly, and condescended to disclose the basis of his rectitude.

" I 'm a — Scout."

" Oh! What 's that got to do with it?"

" Scouts is . . . truthful. That 's a . . . a law."
Norton caught his breath.

" Come on back; I 'll have to play another ball.
So you 're a Scout, are you? What made you
join?"

The boy, trotting swiftly to keep pace with Norton, was ludicrous in his amalgamation of sheepish-
ness and unction.

" Ma did."

" Oh! She did, did she? What for?"

" Said it 'd make me brave."

" Were n't you before?"

" Naw," confessed the Scout, blushing.

" Would n't you fight?"

" *Sure,* but —"

" But what?"

" When I got licked, I . . . I bawled."

Norton, emerging to the fairway, signaled to his
friends, and tossed a ball to the turf.

" Sonny," he said, " I ought to join your troop
myself! Let 's have the heavy midiron!"

The two-stroke penalty gave him a seven for the
long hole; he required two fours and a three for his
coveted seventy-nine. And, to the astonishment
and relief of his associates, he played the first two

of those holes in a mood comparable only to Norton's golfing moods at their highest. Artificiality had gone from him; he was boyishly intent upon his score, but he radiated a new placidity and a dignified resignation which did much to restore the sinking spirits of his loyal mates. The lines receded from his mouth, his eyes betokened retrospective fancies, not of grief; he was the Norton of old, a trifle repressed, but the merest trifle; and the repression was amiable, and complaisant. In particular, his attitude towards his caddy was rather extraordinarily benign; and Hazzard was all the more amazed, because the stupidity of that dirt-encrusted gamin had cost Norton two unnecessary strokes.

Norton got his four, another four, and had the eighteenth left to play, par three for seventy-nine. This terminal hole was two hundred and ten yards, a bothersome carry over the most treacherous of pits — a great crevasse of fine and shifting sand — and it had outposts of lesser pits to guard it. At the rear, there was a shelving bank inclining to a weed-infested pond; to the left, the roadway; and to the right, impenetrable swamps. The wind, which had grown to threatening proportions, swept at right-angles across the line of play, constructively lengthening the distance. Norton wavered, and exhaled stupendously.

" This is the only favor I 've asked," he said. " I do want a three . . . let me drive last. Does anybody mind?"

He was manifestly composed, and his will was indomitable, but no amount of dogma could controvert the fact that he had come to the final hole of the final round. Chance and the wind combined to make it a severer test than he had expected. That hole had become the very apotheosis of golf; it was the ultimate examination of his prowess. And Norton, lingering there under gray skies, a man with fifty thousand holes already scored, and one to play, was shaken not so much by the drama of the hole as by the dramatic value of his own thoughts; he was n't pitying himself as much as he was allowing the justification he had to be pitied. It was, he thought, a smashing, spectacular sort of climax — the scudding clouds, the wind, the frowning pits, the pond — and par three needed for the seventy-nine craved.

Kingsland blundered in sparing the cleek, and Norton leaned far forward to analyze the flight. For a hundred yards the ball engaged to journey far and sure, but of a sudden it was checked, it submitted weakly, it dropped in docile impotence to the hugest pit, twenty degrees off its bearings, and short by a hundred feet.

"More to the left," said Norton half-aloud. "And a full swing."

Peters glowered, and tried the spoon. He was a slugger, Peters, and in playing prepensely to the left, he hit hard from a medium tee; but the ball had not yet reached its fullest height when Norton could predict its landing.

"That's short, too!" he muttered. Indeed, it also buried itself in granular sand.

Hazzard, relying on the brassey, essayed to snatch advantage from the wind, but he used a tee so low that the ball, taking no impertinence from the weather, landed fairly on the green, bounded once and twice, and splashed in the waters of the further pond. It was Norton's shot.

As he advanced to drive, he was attacked by a convulsive twitching of the muscles which brought him near to apoplexy. The entire purport of his undertaking was centered on this paramount eighteenth hole; he had seen three well-hit drives fall into trouble; he had seen what unparagoned execution was demanded of a man who would hole his putt for a model three. And Norton longed for that card of seventy-nine; he had adjured himself that if, in his sore predicament, he could break eighty for this pregnant round, he would be content. To break eighty was to triumph over mind and body; it would salve his coming disability, and give oblivion a cud to chew on. And to a man of his mature attainments, a dreadful gulf lies between seventy-nine and eighty; it is a difference which no layman can find transparent; but to a golfer it represents a variation tenfold greater than its arithmetic. It seemed to him that never since he was born had he yearned for anything as now he yearned for that all but insuperable par.

Beyond the pit, and verging to the confines of the green, there was an arid quarter acre of pebbly soil. Ladies and timorous men of 18-handicap played conspicuously for it, and used a niblick for the second shot, and not infrequently arrived at the tin in four. Norton, if unadventurous, could get an eighty; he would have wagered every penny of his resources that he could do no worse. If he used wood, and overdrove, like Hazzard, he could foresee no better fortune than five for an eighty-one. If he were bold, but fraternized with Peters and Kingsland in the sand, he might conceivably take five, or six, or seven, since the pit was craftily constructed, both in shape and substance. So that Norton's talent was on trial, and his acumen as well; he must elect his policy, and take a certain four, or chance his three, and run the risk of strokes unlimited in number. And as he balanced one alternative against the other, the dead weight of the crisis fell upon and harrowed him. He was in a ghastly quandary; the intrinsic value of that eighteen hole as a criterion of golf was trivial in comparison with its emphasis as a meridian. It was the culmination of fifty thousand holes.

Norton glanced at his caddy, who was disputing vigorously but inaudibly with his chums.

"Better play safe, Billy," said Kingsland.

"Aw, I betcha!" shrilled Norton's caddy, stung to resonance.

"Boy!" snapped Peters ominously.

"He ain't no quitter! A nickel he gets a three!"

"*Caddy!*" roared Kingsland.

"Brassey," said Norton. "Give me the brassey."

A chorus of protests rose in opposition.

"Billy — don't! Play it safe!"

"You'll have to sky it — and listen to that wind!"

"Play short, Billy — use common-sense! Take your eighty! That's good enough!"

"Brassey," said Norton, pluckily. "If it's the last hole I'll ever play, I'm going to play it right."

His voice contained the least imaginable tremor;

but his heart was pounding precariously, and for
the first time this afternoon, he was physically
racked — so wrung with torment that, as he took
his stance, he doubted if he could even swing the
club. Lights danced before his eyes, and roaring
echoes filled his ears; he had no stomach, and his
arms and wrists and shoulders quaked in synchro-
nism with his knees. The wind was tugging
strongly at his coat; he felt powerless to withstand
it by any effort of his own. The green was so very,
very distant. . . . Norton gulped, and dried his
palms on his handkerchief.

What he wanted was a three, no more, no less.
A four would satisfy him no better than a seven, or
a seventeen. He had published his intention to
break eighty, and until he had played his seventy-
ninth stroke without holding out, he would still
direct his inexorable perseverance to that one resolve. But struggle as he would, Norton could n't
separate himself from the tragedy which was crushing him with every clock-tick. The desperate catastrophe of the thing was what unmanned him; after
this eighteenth hole he was through with golf, ex-
patriated, superannuated. He was to be torn in-
continently from his passion; he was condemned to
be at best a listener, and a raconteur. He, the general who had harkened to the applause of a multi-

tude, was reduced to the ranks; he was swaying on the last tee, he had teed the last ball, he was facing the last hole. A choking sob caught in his throat, and lead was in his breast. He was strangled, suffocated; and, concurrently, nauseated by the tumult within himself.

" This is the . . . the finish," he whispered.

He drew an imaginary line to the left of the green, and gave the wind the benefit of another point; he teed periculously high. Then judgment failed him, and his motor impulses assumed authority. He addressed the ball; confirmed his direction; smiled with a curiously repulsive grimace; and swung; and as his body completed the follow-through, he dropped the club because his hands were no longer able to hold it. He had reached the uttermost limit of his endurance.

The ball, against a background of lofty trees, was flying geometrically to the line. It was billeted for the road, and out of bounds, unless a miracle intervened, and Hazzard, white-lipped, raised his hand in quite involuntary supplication.

" She's coming around!" yelled Peters, snatching at Kingsland's elbow.

" You're *on!* " bawled Kingsland, tearing himself loose.

"Look!" said Hazzard, pointing shakily. "L — look — look —!"

"Look!" said Hazzard, pointing shakily. "L-look . . . look . . .!"

The ball had landed ten yards short, and ricochetted towards the hole; slower and slower it spun; it brought up against the pin, caromed off, and lay there, glistening in the pale sunlight six inches from the cup.

Three frenzied maniacs surrounded Norton, pumping his hand and howling incoherent delight. Forgetful of his weakness — and he himself forgot it for a time — they pummeled him until he cried for mercy.

"You almost got a *one!*" shrieked Hazzard. "A *one!* You missed it an *inch!*"

"A wonderful shot — wonderful!"

"Let him alone — let him alone!" pleaded Kingsland. "He's got a putt yet — come on!"

They raced down towards the pits as rapidly as Norton could run — afterwards he realized that he had been foolhardy, but this was no occasion for squeamishness. They gained the green, and saw that Norton's ball was a narrow hand's breadth from the haven of the hole.

"I — I never made a one in my life," he said ecstatically.

"I *wish* you'd got it!" mourned Hazzard. "But, my Lord!"

"I don't," said Norton, transported. "I'd — it would have been a *horrible* fluke —"

"And instead of that," put in Kingsland excitedly, "it was just a beautiful, beautiful drive. . . ."

"It's a discreeminating seventy-eight," said Peters.

Norton guffawed feverishly.

"Not yet, I — I may miss the putt!"

"Yes — it's likely!"

"Take your time, Billy! Sink it, now!"

"Just a minute," said Norton. He walked impetuously to the grinning boy who had sponsored him and insured his victory. "Now then, caddy," said Norton, "loan me your putter, will you? One putt, and I'll give it back to you." He broke out laughing at the boy's bewilderment. "I won't ever need 'em any more," he added. "They're yours — and there's some balls in the pocket, too. You can call it your war cross if you want to . . . don't look so rattled. . . . I'm making you a present . . . now loan me that putter!"

And tapped the ball for his seventy-eight, and a birdie to close the chapter.

In the clubhouse, when Norton was reclining,

woefully exhausted in a leather chair, and avowing to himself that the doctors were indubitably sound in their decree, Hazzard came to him, and clasped his hand tightly, and showed by the futility of his speech what affection he had for Norton.

"But I'd give anything I own," he concluded, "to have seen you make a one on that last hole. I would, really."

Norton smiled in the beatitude of golden reminiscence.

"Well, Bunker," he said, languidly, "that's one way of looking at it — but consider the other side. It's all over — *finis coronat* Norton! And when I think about it, I can remember always and always that I wound up with a birdie . . . and nothing could be pleasanter than that. But . . . well, how'd *you* feel if you'd been in my shoes to-day? As it is, people will know I broke eighty. I had n't played for weeks and weeks, and I was n't very fit — and I broke eighty. That's all they'll say. I broke eighty. And . . . how would it be if people said: 'Hear about Billy Norton's finish? Luck of the devil, was n't it? *But he always was lucky, was n't he?*'"

"Then . . . then you must have *wanted* that ball to stay out of the cup . . . when it was coming so close. That's funny. I —"

"I prayed for it to stay out," said Norton simply. "I prayed for it . . . *a one is n't golf!*" He leaned back wearily, and closed his eyes. Hazzard, after a moment, moved stealthily away. A mile to the northward, a tousled caddy was displaying a kit of clubs in a wondrous bag to a mother who was charmed and proud, and most inquisitive.

"But *why?*" she persisted. "What d' you *do?* He must 'a' had *some* reason."

"I dunno," said the caddy, reciprocally dazzled and nonplussed. "I dunno. He 's a peacherino — he shot a seventy-eight. *I* did n't do nothin'. He just give 'em to me!"

IF IT INTERFERES WITH
BUSINESS

IF Mr. Horatio Baring had n't got out of the
wrong side of bed that morning — subsequent to
crawling into it on the same side the night before —
the attitude of his first visitor and client would certainly have charmed him and renewed his confidence
in a vacillating administration. The client was val-
iantly optimistic in a bear market. He alleged that
the country was on the verge of boom prosperity
which, by its creation of a fresh set of multi-million-
aires, would set Henry Ford back to a rating of
second credit, and place the Bread Line on a level
with the Draft Riots as an unpleasant historical fact
almost impossible to believe; and he declared further that at the present state of affairs the bonds of
Quito Copper at 112, when, as and if issued, were
even as money found on the sidewalk, shouting
loudly for help. Since Mr. Baring was informally
associated with the members of the syndicate which
was distributing those highly speculative securities,
and knew that just at this moment 110¼ and an
oath of fealty were sufficient to bring them promptly

across the counter to a friend like himself, there was apparently little reason for the remarkable restraint he displayed at this juncture. Nothing in the code of ethics of the Stock Exchange would have prevented him from smiling and bringing out his best mulatto cigars and excusing himself to speak briefly in a hushed voice over the wire, at a resultant gross profit to himself of a good point and three quarters.

But the smile of Mr. Baring had recently congealed under the weathering of his frosty thought. It was in his capacity of parent, and not banker, that he looked upon the world this morning; and as a parent he nurtured a soul in revolt, and it hurt him exceedingly.

For a synopsis: There was a certain young man who, in the early winter, had once taken the most accommodating of all the electric trains from New York to call upon Miss Margaret Baring in the suburbs; and on that first occasion the parent had said: "Kenyon? Harry Kenyon? He's with Garfield and Porter. Why, we do a lot of business with his house, but he's a man I don't admire . . . he doesn't seem to have any sense of responsibility. Plays golf on week days . . . golf! Think of it; week days! Met him at a dance, I suppose? . . . Well, I should say a dancing broker is just about the

sort of man I 'd *expect* to play golf, come to think
of it!"

The third time he had laughed shortly and said:
"Kenyon again? What 's he done — bought a
commutation ticket? I tell you, a man who wastes
the time *he* does could n't get a job in *my* office!
Crack amateur golfer! . . . A crack amateur golfer
does n't belong anywhere but in a golf club! . . . *I*
want to do business with crack professional bankers!"

And the sixth time he had said: "What 's that
cub hanging around here for all the time? Has n't
he any home?"

And last night he had stated fluently, and without
the tact you might reasonably expect from one who
lived on commissions: "Look here, Peggy, this
thing has got to stop!" To which Miss Baring had
rejoined with gentle emphasis: "I 'm sorry if you
don't like Harry, father . . . it 's too bad, because
I think we 're going to be married before so *very*
long."

He had stared at her in a species of icy indigna-
tion which astonished them equally. His daughter!
. . . the daughter he had intended some time — oh,
so *very* some time! — to marry a conservative, well-
established, reputable member of the Exchange, had
spoken mutinously of allying herself with a wild

Harvard graduate who still drew a salary and played good golf — circumstantial evidence of a misspent youth!

" Do you take me for an *idiot?* " he had gasped.

" Well," Peggy had responded dreamily, " I don't see what *that* has to do with it —"

So for two grinding hours they had interrupted each other and despatched hundreds of trains of thought which never reached their destination, and exchanged widely diverging views on the character of young men who neglect commerce in favor of sport, and on middle-aged men who don't appreciate sport because in temperament they were already grandfathers when they were born; and Mr. Baring had said that if Peggy truly loved him, she'd promptly forget this whipper-snapper who wasn't in any sense worthy of her; and Peggy had said in rebuttal that if Mr. Baring truly loved *her,* he wouldn't stand in the way of her happiness; and then they had kissed, and inquired in the same breath if the other were convinced. It was about as conclusive as a friendly argument between a rabid suffragist and a violent anti; except that there was no tea.

Presently Mr. Baring had gone to bed with a headache, indigestion, and the lassitude of anemia; and he had spent the major part of the night in

"I am sorry if you don't like Harry   .   .   .'

wondering, after the manner of fathers taken by surprise in the presence of individuality, if Peggy would have been more docile if she had been spanked oftener when she was young.

So that even the potentiality of nearly two per cent. for merely telephoning around the corner could n't wring a smile from Mr. Baring in the morning.

" If you can get 'em by eleven o'clock at 112 or better," said the ingenuous client, lighting one of his own cigars, " I 'll take twenty-five — and if you can shade the price by three eighths or a half, I 'll take twenty thousand more for my wife."

" Just a minute," said Mr. Baring, looking the wraith of a thousand dollar profit full in the face and never batting an eye.

He went personally to a booth in the outer office and called a number, then a name.

" Hello! " he said.   " This Barton?   Hello, Hal. This is Baring. . . . How 's Quito? . . . No; I mean the bonds. . . . Oh, of course, ten and a half bid on the Curb, but that was my own bid! . . . Yes; for a customer . . . none of it came out. . . . How about forty-five to me direct? . . . forty-five thousand; that 's right . . . well, you don't mean that Kenyon controls all the rest of your allotment.

do you? . . . Is that so? . . . I did n't realize they were going that fast. . . . On his own account? . . . Well, can I speak to him? . . . Well, when do you expect him? . . . I 'll hold the wire." He leaned wearily against the frame of the booth and wondered what a heart-sick man could do with a thousand dollars out of the sky. Something for Peggy, most likely — he might even add a bit to the windfall and present her with a trip to San Francisco or Japan —

"Hello! Yes . . . what? . . . *he won't be back to-day! He's out playing golf! . . . Where?*"

There was a pause. Mr. Baring drew a long breath, took the receiver carefully, hung it on the hook, and stepped out into the customers' room. A junior clerk glanced at him and hurried forward.

"Are you ill, sir? Can I do anything for you?"

"You call the Garden City Golf Club and have 'em bring Harry Kenyon in to talk to me — he's playing in some fool tournament out there. Have 'em tell him it 's real business — it 's important!"

He drank a glass of water and dropped into a leather chair to await the answer. Suddenly he felt very old and lackadaisical; he told himself that in the future there must be no repetition of last night's melodramatic performance; the loss of sleep told too heavily upon him. Besides, his nerves were n't what they once had been; his hands, he observed, were unsteady. Lately, too, he had known intervals of dizziness after breakfast. . . . Perhaps he might do well to appropriate that thousand dollars for a little vacation for himself and Peggy. He thought that in the Adirondacks or in almost any region far enough distant from the confusion of the city. . . . Here his revery was rudely broken, and he was alert again.

"I 'm sorry, sir," deprecated the clerk; "they won't call him." The clerk, incidentally, was a 20-handicap man, and in secret he had rather contemned his employer for his ignorance of to-day's event.

"They — they *won't* call him? Did they actually tell you they would n't?" Mr. Baring went apoplectic, and both his hands wandered out in aimless gestures.

"No, sir. You see, it 's the qualifying round of the Metropolitan — he went out in 37, by the way — and he left word that he would n't take any business messages at all during the day. But it 's doubtful if they 'd have taken the chance of disqualifying him, anyway."

"I think," said Mr. Baring, turning that popular

shade known as Russian green, " you 'd better —
send for somebody. . . . I don't feel — quite well."
He smiled limply; it was his valediction to the thousand dollars he had resolved to spend for recreation.
" Golf," he added vacuously, " golf, Jimmy, is a —
a damned — expensive — game — for me . . . and
I don't play it . . . either! "

Then darkness and the inevitable result of two
tremendous moral explosions after thirty years in
Wall Street without a moment's relaxation.

At Garden City, over on Long Island, young Mr.
Kenyon sank a long and tricky putt for a par four,
and did n't remotely suspect how the course of true
love was running.

The Barings' touring car, Miss Baring at the
wheel, swerved from the Post Road and slipped
quietly along the shaded private avenue which led
to the Norwood Golf Club. By her side Mr. Horatio Baring, stiff-backed and unrelenting, squinted at
a solitary duffer practising iron shots on the eight-
eenth-hole fairway. The duffer, hearing the purr
of the motor, naturally began to exaggerate his
swing so as to conform to the familiar bronze of
Vardon, and naturally dubbed a few.

" There are times," said Mr. Baring gloomily,
" when I 'm about ready to believe the whole

world's in its second childhood. This is one of them." He inspected the façade of the clubhouse with the enthusiasm of one approaching Ossining for involuntary residence. "If these young asses would only go to hoeing potatoes —"

"Oh, you've promised, and I'm not going to let you back out of it," said Peggy cheerfully, as she brought the car to a standstill in the parking circle. "There is n't any other outdoor exercise you can take — now, *is* there? You're not strong enough. And if you hoed potatoes, think of your social standing!"

Mr. Baring, not condescending to reply, disembarked in silence, and suffered himself to be led to the lobby and registered as a guest. Later, when he stood by the first tee and stared at a scratch foursome, he remarked loudly: "It's on the same principle as most things; if I'd been a paying teller instead of a banker, I'd have been satisfied to walk to work and buy a croquet set. Or eat some pills. Well — what do I do?"

"Sh-h-h!" said Miss Baring sharply.

One of the foursome hooked out of bounds, and looked first in sorrow at the face of his club and then in accusation at Mr. Baring.

"This is a fine game!" scorned the banker in a hoarse whisper. "I can imagine somebody saying

Sh-h-h! at the Polo Grounds when Tris Speaker comes to the bat! Why don't you all wear muzzles and put me on a leash? . . . Well, they're off — what do I do?"

"I thought probably you'd better just walk around with me this afternoon," said Peggy, "to get an idea of the game. There's no use beginning until you know the object of it. Then to-morrow you can take a lesson. Now be still a second — I'm going to drive."

She took several practice swings, after each of which her father made a false start forward, and was deterred by the caddy; then she sliced badly, the ball hopping a high bunker.

"Over the fence — good shot!" appreciated Mr. Baring. "What does that count?"

She was still involved in explanations when they reached the rough, and the minutes she occupied in coercing the ball back to the course were mere interludes subtracted from the full measure of her lecture.

"Is this all there is to it?" demanded Mr. Baring as Peggy eventually holed in eight. "Then what's the sense of lugging around all those overgrown dentist's tools? Plain bluff?"

Peggy reverted to first principles.

"Well, every hole is different —"

"All right; show me another," he requested patiently.

She displayed no remarkable skill on the second hole, but on the third she ran down a twenty-foot putt for a four, and turned innocently for the applause. To her amazement, her father was yawning.

"Why, *father!*" she chided. "That was an *awfully* good shot!"

"Was it?" he asked indifferently.

"Well, if you think it's so easy, let's see *you* try it!"

To humor her, he grasped the club she gave him and approximated the distance.

"I don't see how you can miss it," scoffed Mr. Baring, indulgently; and allowing not an inch for the undulations, or for a worm cast or two, he rapped the ball smartly and watched it disappear, with a satisfying rattle, into the cup. "There!" he said. "What's simpler?"

"Wonderful!" she cried. "Perfect! Your very first shot, too! That's wonderful! Now let's see what you can do with a wooden club!" Mightily pleased and only normally wicked, she presented him with a driver, which he handled thoughtfully.

"I see," he admitted. "You use a little stick for

the short hits and a heavy bat for the long ones. All right. Watch her sail!" He set himself, gritted his teeth, raised his whole body with the club, smashed at the ball, grunted "*Whoof!*" and sent a screaming drive straight down the course for two hundred and twenty yards. "What a kindergarten game!" he commented pompously. "And that fool doctor calls this *exercise!* Why, I can knock it a mile!"

His daughter, swinging vigorously, came to even terms with him after her third shot.

"Want to try a brassey?" she asked.

"I'll try anything once." He struck awry, and topped.

"Oh, too bad!" she sympathized.

"Now, look here!" said Mr. Baring with some asperity. "I know a little more about athletics than you think I do! It doesn't make any difference whether you put a line drive over second or a grounder between third and short — they both count for safe hits! That was a grounder — it's rolling yet! All I need is a couple more like that, and I'll plant it right in the can."

"Hole," she groaned.

"Whatever you call it," he conceded pleasantly, "I'll be in it." Nevertheless, for the following ten minutes he was plowing so diligently through tall grass, and foozling so often, that when he came to the green he was counting in double figures. "Oh, that can't be bad for a beginner," was his extenuation. "I've had four safe ones out of twelve. That's what they'd call batting for .300 in the big leagues. Nobody can poke fun at *that?* Where's the light stick?"

They were overtaken at this point by a mutual friend, who expressed joy at the meeting and astonishment at the geography of it. He himself, he submitted, was off his game entirely; he had recorded even sevens for the first two holes, and then relapsed into mediocrity. Might he join them?

"Come on in," invited the banker. "If I had some sticks of my own instead of this child's-size outfit, and if my shoes weren't so slippery, and I hadn't been down in that gully back there, and —"

"You're learning," grinned the friend. "I had a chance for a five on the third, and I'd have made it if I'd had my regular niblick."

"You missed something, not seeing my first hit," Mr. Baring told him. "On the Polo Grounds it would have been clean out in the center-field bleachers. And if they'd only get some laborers to clear the rocks out —"

"I almost always get a five on the second hole," insisted the friend. "But to-day —"

"Where's the next link? Say, is n't this club solvent? There's a half-acre of sand back there that ought to be grassed over. Is it my turn? What does it count if I hit the flagpole?"

He did n't. But he did hit a tree.

At the ninth hole Miss Baring professed weariness, and suggested a halt. Her father, however, was opposed. He stated warmly that golf required hardly more exertion than bridge, and that it was n't his policy to default in the middle of a rubber. The full round was what he intended to accomplish.

"You 'll blister your hands," she prophesied.

"That's all right! Wallace's beaten me only two to one, and we two tied — you let me take your sticks and I 'll finish the game. If I only had a good, heavy Louisville slugger, *I* 'd show you some pinch-hitting! You sit down and wait for us. Come on, Wallace! It's your licks!"

Accordingly, Miss Baring strolled into the clubhouse, where she encountered young Mr. Kenyon, and straightway strolled out again to a corner of the glassed-in veranda.

"Father's here," she said. "Is n't it funny?"
Kenyon lifted his eyebrows.
"*Playing?*"
"Yes; it 's his first day. They made him."

"That's great!" said Kenyon. "He needs it."

"Well, his breakdown frightened him more than he lets us think. I finally persuaded him to play golf, but he's certainly made a terrible fuss about it, and I had to get a regular injunction from his doctor, too. It's taken me two solid weeks to get him out here."

"Has he — changed his mind at all?"

"About you? No-o-o, I'm afraid he has n't. You see, he was prejudiced in the beginning, and then when he lost that big commission because you were at Garden City, he was perfectly furious — it was n't the money, but the principle, you know — and it happened to come just when he was most upset anyway —"

"Obviously," said Kenyon, "he does n't see *my* side of it. *I* did n't lose anything — in fact, I made money by not being in town that day. Twenty-four hours afterward I sold at 115 — and I got up to the semifinals in the Metropolitan. I suppose that does n't interest him."

Peggy shook her head.

"No, I don't imagine it does."

"But I wonder," said Kenyon reflectively, "if he'll change his ideas after he's played for a while."

"I'd thought of that — and I was tremendously pleased to see how excited he got when he won a hole from Mr. Wallace. Of course, I would n't dare to tell him that Mr. Wallace is easily ten strokes worse than the next worst player in the club. That would n't mean anything to him, anyhow. As a matter of fact, I don't remember that he's ever played any game before in his whole life. About once a month he goes to a baseball match, and that's as much of a sportsman as he's been. He thinks games are silly. But if he once gets the fever —"

"A hole in par," said Kenyon. "Or two or three fine shots in succession."

"Yes — why, that would be an awfully good thing for him and for us, too."

"Do you think he'd like to have me coach him? If I could help him at all —"

Her negative was immediate and forceful.

"Don't! Please don't try! He would n't understand. And it *might* make him all the more furious to see you doing so well. There's nothing for us to do, except to wait — and plan."

While waiting they planned with such absorption that it was heavy dusk before Miss Baring awoke to consciousness of the hour.

"Perhaps," she suggested, a little anxiously, "I'd better go out after them."

"We'll go together," said Kenyon.

From the veranda of the club they could overlook the entire sweep of the eighteenth hole and part of the treacherous seventeenth. Mr. Baring and his partner were n't in sight; so that the young people went over to the plateau of the sixteenth green and from this eminence surveyed the landscape in all directions. A stone's throw to the south, in the dismal swamp which penalizes a poor tee shot, they faintly discerned two figures toiling in the gloom. Breathless, they strained their eyes towards the devoted pair.

" This sort of job," came to them in Mr. Baring's impressive baritone, " is what made General Goethals famous!"

" Hush!" whispered Peggy. " Don't let them see us! Come back under the trees!"

" That 's nine for you," shrilled Wallace's voice, as his opponent dug viciously into the bed of the winding creek. " I 'm over in twelve."

" That 's *eight* for me —"

" It can't be. You were three getting off the tee; one back of the bushes; two in the mud; then a good out —"

" One in the mud," disputed Mr. Baring. " Only one, and the *next* was the good one — and I 'll be hanged if I see how you 're over in twelve! You said you were ten behind that rock —"

"Nine. And then I —"

"Please don't talk when I'm getting ready to bat!"

After a brief pause: "That's nine anyway," said Wallace complacently. "Ten. . . . Eleven. . . . Twelve. . . . Thir — Oh, good out!"

"A corker," granted Mr. Baring. "I'll tell you just how I did it —"

"Never mind! I'll get this hole yet!"

"You'll have to play your head off! And if *I* get it, I'll be one ahead."

"Well, if I had my regular midiron —"

"Midiron! I don't even know what a midiron looks ·like, but how can I play with a *girl's* clubs! And I'd be ahead now if you counted straight —"

"Well, all I was going to say was that if I had a decent sheepskin grip on my midiron, I wouldn't have been in the swamp at all! I can carry that nine times out of ten against the wind."

"Like fun you could! That's a joke — that is! That's slapstick comedy! I'll bet you never drove clear over that swamp in your life!"

"I'll carry it nine times out of ten, on a bet — with my regular midiron!"

"Well, are you going to shoot, or are you going to stay here all night?"

"I'll shoot soon enough. You've played two more —"

"Two more than what? You? I certainly have *not!* We're even!"

"I'm twelve to here, and you're —"

"I'm twelve myself! Go ahead and play! . . . Rotten! . . . and that's thirteen for you by your own count!"

"How in thunder can I hit it when you yell at me just as I start to swing! . . . There! Look at that! Now *why* don't you say something funny? Go on — pull some more of your Broad Street humor! Where'd it land?"

"You're in the pit! Now I'll show you a *good* shot!"

Another pause, followed by one imprecation and one gurgle of delight.

"You're in the pit, too! If I had my old niblick — the one I was telling you about — I could lay it right up to the pin. I can't do anything with this one —"

"Oh, pumpernickel! The only way you could get out of that trench in one shot is with a load of dynamite!"

"Is that so!"

From the pit, twin puffs, as of rifle smoke, rose and drifted away on the evening breeze.

"Fourteen!" said Mr. Baring exultantly.

"Thirteen!" said Mr. Wallace stubbornly.

"You 're wrong!" they said in chorus; and during the ensuing lull two more puffs rose and dissipated.

Miss Baring and Kenyon, ambushed in the orchard by the green, turned to each other and smiled.

"I guess it 's all right," murmured Peggy beatifically.

"He 's inoculated," said Kenyon. His arm went around her, and in the twilight their lips met.

"Eighteen — and I 'm in!" roared Mr. Baring. "Now I 'm one ahead! — and it 's the first day I ever had a club in my hands! Don't we call the game off on account of darkness? Who 's the umpire in a situation like this? It 's too dark to play any more."

"Two to go," said Mr. Wallace grimly. "Get out there, caddy, and mark the ball! The game 's over when it 's finished. There 's a young pond sixty yards ahead, Baring — take my advice and use a floater, and play short anyway. All right. One down and two to go. A dollar on the match?"

"Ten," said Mr. Baring rashly. "But if I only had the right kind of shoes, so I would n't be slipping and sliding every minute —"

By the first of August his case was serious. He owned a bag with so many patent clubs of base metal that only the older boys were physically able to caddy for him; and his theories were heavier than his irons. He took three lessons a week from the Norwood professional; and rehearsed by the hour the orthodox swing, with the hands well under the shaft; he went out on the course feeling like a Scotch internationalist at plus six; and he came limping back in the gloaming with a card full of sevens and eights, and spoke hoarsely in the grill-room of what miracles he should perform to-morrow. Half an ounce of lead in his brassey, he judged, and a quarter inch removed from the length of his cleek, ought to bring about an improvement of a dozen strokes at the minimum. And if it were n't a question of weight, or of balance, it was a matter of ivory facing, or perhaps a slight modification of the position of his left thumb. At any rate, he was fertile in invention.

He bought all of the forty-seven standard books on golf, and read them from cover to cover, propping them open at every illustration, and posturing according to the diagrams. In addition, he read everything that Rice and Anderson had to say in the newspapers, and by these methods of indirect instruction he learned all about torsional strain and the least beneficial alternative, and slowly acquired a technical vocabulary of some elasticity and power. He experimented with every known make of ball and every fetish of stance and grip. He kept all his practice cards; that is, all those which showed medal scores within two strokes of his lowest record; for when he was beyond that modest margin he complained that he was off his game, and confessed that the day was spoiled. And, together with fifty other members of the club, he signed the insurgent's petition to the grounds committee to fill in the brook hazard on the fourteenth, because it was unfair to a long driver, although a proper penalty for a second shot. He signed it without conceit, for once he had hit a ball which bounded within thirty yards of the brook, so that he knew exactly how the long drivers felt about that hazard, and agreed with them.

But in spite of his advancement and his ardor, he still remained adamant in his pristine aversion to Kenyon.

Long ago he had forbidden that astonished young man the house; he would have also forbidden him the golf club if any original jurisdiction had been vested in him. Not even the result of the local championship, during which Kenyon never played the last three holes, save in the qualifying round, tempered his determination; and the shattering of the amateur record moved him not at all. Indeed, he seemed to dislike Kenyon all the more.

Yet it seems incredible that Mr. Baring could have enjoyed such continuing ignorance of the facts. For one thing, the steady improvement in Peggy's game should have warned him; the smooth wrist action which Harry Kenyon alone of the local players had mastered, or could impart; the snappy mashie pitch which is controlled by not more than one woman in a hundred — or one man, for that matter; the bold, deliberate running up of long putts — all these should have penetrated Mr. Baring's intelligence, and helped him to the deduction that Peggy was playing far too often with Kenyon.

Instead, the revelation was sudden and shocking; he found them together playing cut shots out of a trap; and at the moment of discovery he was already four down to Wallace, and had broken a hollow-faced cleek in trying to pull off a wind cheater.

Furthermore, he had topped into the same trap.

Kenyon, who was lecturing, looked up instinctively and saw the irate parent tottering on the summit of the worst bunker on the course. The parent's face, already dyed with the carmine of vexation, went brick-red with anger; and he boiled with bitterness at the realization that his daughter's conduct could make him feel so bitter. If he had obeyed the spontaneous demands of his fury, he would have slain Kenyon with a deep-faced mashie where he stood. As it was, restrained by civilization, and yet goaded by his atavistic desires, he merely spluttered.

Miss Baring, magnetized by the electric silence, also turned her head, and blanched.

" *Well!* " said Mr. Baring.

" Is this your ball? " asked Kenyon, indicating.

" Yes," said the irate parent, shaking with emotion. " That is my ball . . . that is my ball . . . *that is my ball. . . .*"

" Tough luck," said Kenyon. " But now you've got to pull off exactly the shot I'm teaching Peggy. Come on down and I'll show you how to make it."

" Young man," roared Mr. Baring, striding forward, " young man, when I come to *you* for advice —"

Here his feet slipped on the bunker's rim, and he was unexpectedly sitting in the trap, jarred to silence. Tears stood in his eyes; he coddled his tongue in anguish. .

" Now that you've come," said Keynon, requisitioning a club from Mr. Baring's caddy. " Take this!" He dragged Peggy's father upright.

" Stand ahead of it, Mr. Baring . . . put one foot here and the other one *here!* . . . no, ahead of it more . . . much farther; farther yet — take it back with the right . . . cut across *here* when you come down . . . that's the idea! Now go for it!"

The banker, speechless, baffled, outraged, and just a trifle under the hypnotic influence — perhaps he had seen the revival of " Trilby " that week — played out of the trap. In fact, he got more distance out of the sand than he was in the habit of getting off the fair. For a moment he gaped in wonder; then he remembered that he was irate, and that he had n't delivered his oral message.

" Now, young man," he began ominously, " let me tell you —"

" Let me tell *you*," said Kenyon, " that if you get off half your shots with that same precision, you 'll be playing around in the low nineties by October."

" Good digging," ventured Peggy, softly. " A lovely shot, dad! Do another!"

Mr. Baring, perceiving that neither of the young people was alarmed, and furthermore, that Wallace was wrestling desperately in a thicket, breathed less heavily.

" Do you — do you think it's honorable for you to come out here like this — after the last conversation we had, Kenyon? To make clandestine appointments —"

"I certainly do, Mr. Baring. We're both over twenty-one. And on Saturdays this trap is about as clandestine as the Grand Central Terminal in the rush hour!"

Over in the hay field Wallace was playing nine.

"I'm glad to know you think so — because at least that infers a clear conscience. But do you mean to say that you haven't deliberately taken advantage of me? Can you say that and expect me to believe it?"

"I can say it — I *do* say it. But I'm not responsible for what you think. Incidentally, we've never made an appointment to play together — if we've chanced to meet, we've gone out —"

Mr. Baring appealed to his daughter.

"Is that true, Peggy?"

"Of course it is! Didn't he say so?"

"To that extent I credit you with good intentions," said Mr. Baring with dignity which was somewhat impaired by an impulse to touch with his forefinger the tongue he had bitten when he sat down.

Over in the meadow Wallace had lost his ball.

"Don't you want to try another shot?" inquired Kenyon. "There's plenty of time."

After a momentary tensity, the financier burst out laughing.

"I'll also credit you with plenty of gall, Kenyon."

"You need it in this game," said the younger man ambiguously.

"Let's play around with them," proposed Miss Baring. "Mr. Wallace won't mind, and I'm sure you could help father a lot."

"It's for you to say," hesitated Kenyon.

Mr. Baring's shoulders were squared in military fashion; and his mouth was implacable.

"If you understand that such a concession does n't carry with it a retraction of anything I said to you three months ago," he conceded, "I have no valid objection to making up a foursome. In fact I think I should prefer it under the present circumstances."

As they moved away Kenyon walked at his elbow.

"Mr. Baring," he said, "*why* should you have objected to my playing golf? You play yourself now — and you 're out here oftener than I am; and you 're in the same business —"

"*I*," responded the banker hastily, "am under the instructions of a physician."

" You 're still angry about that day when I was playing in the Metropolitan? "

Mr. Baring nodded affirmatively.

" I still think you were very discourteous to me."

" Have you ever stopped to think that, even if I 'd been in town that day, I might not have sold you any bonds at *your* figure? "

Mr. Baring sniffed sharply.

" The point is n't that I lost a profit — and, as an aftermath, a customer — but that your action was unbusinesslike and uncivil. You should have come to the telephone when I asked for you."

" Even though I made money by not coming? "

" I fail to see how that affects me! "

" Some men might see the connection."

" The incident, as it stands —"

" The incident, as it stands, simply confirms the truth of my statement that one of us had a chance to make money. I got there first."

" Now, look here," said Mr. Baring testily. " If you want to argue this out, you can come to my office any week-day during office hours and I 'll give you a hearing. That is, any day but Tuesday and Friday. This is n't any place to talk over family affairs. I 'm four down to here. If you can think out any logical excuse, I 'll listen to it. What would you use next — an iron? "

"Jigger," advised Kenyon. "Let me show you —" . . .

The dramatics of commercial life are usually staged without rehearsal or due regard to climax. One morning in early September the senior partner of Kenyon's firm sent for him and fired a bombshell in these pleasant terms:

"Harry, they've cabled from Yokohama for one of our New York men to rush out there in a hurry — they're up against it, hard. It'll take somewhere between three and six months. We've picked you. You're the only man who isn't tied down. You'll have to catch the Wolverine this afternoon. I've wired for your accommodation on the Santa Fé right through; and you'll have eight hours in San Francisco before your boat sails. If you make good out there, I'm afraid we'll have to let you buy a partnership for not much money. If you can be ready by three o'clock, I'll meet you at the Biltmore with all the data and some letters."

Kenyon grimaced, and brightened.

"How about expenses?"

"Same as usual. We take your vouchers at face value."

Kenyon wavered.

"Suppose I want expenses for two?"

" What 's the graft? "

" I might be married about noon. I 'll let you know in a few minutes."

" That 's all right — we 'll take care of you this time, only you 'll have to speed it up, old man! "

Whereupon Kenyon went back to his own room and called Miss Baring.

" Oh! " she cried. " *Japan!* "

" On a wedding trip," said Kenyon. " Free! There 'll never be another chance like it! And there won't be time enough for you to stock up here, but you 'll have half a day in Chicago and half a day in San Francisco to buy all the clothes in the world. Just take a kit bag, or a steamer trunk, or something, and meet me —"

" But — but *father!* " she gasped.

" I 'm going straight over to see him now."

" But if he —"

" I 'll guarantee that he won't put any obstacles in our way — you leave that to me, Peggy! All you 've got to do is to get to New York — I have an old running mate who 's assistant minister at Grace Church — what train can you catch? "

" Oh, Harry! " she faltered. " If he *should* object —"

" He won't say a word," Kenyon assured her.

"You let me handle that part of it. Will you come?"

" Y-yes, but —"

" What train?"

" There's one due at half past twelve —"

" I'll meet you. Can you pick out a ring in fifteen minutes?"

" Y-yes — but, *Harry* — it's so *sudden!*"

" Chestnut!" he laughed. " And it's just as sudden for me as it is for you — yes, I'll meet you! — *good-by!*"

On his way to the street he poked his head into the senior partner's sanctum and reported: " Expenses for two!" Then he raced to the cab stand, jumped into the first car in line, and ordered a lawless journey around the corner.

Although it was ten-thirty of a week-day morning, Mr. Baring wasn't in. The switchboard operator said that he hadn't been in, and that she had no means of knowing when he would be in. On request she called his major club, his minor clubs, and the golf club. There was no trace of Mr. Baring.

" Try his house," urged Kenyon impatiently. " Ask if they know where I can find him!"

It appeared that he had breakfasted at seven and departed without leaving an itinerary.

" Well," puzzled Kenyon, " where *would* he be? " The operator denied omniscience, and remarked that New York was a large and growing city. " Anyway," he directed, " call every place you can think of where he *might* be! This is important! "

He looked at his watch; it was already eleven o'clock. He had five hours in which to pack mobilia for a transcontinental journey, to soothe a parent and marry a daughter, to receive instructions, and to set forth. To any but a cosmopolitan it would have seemed quick action. Kenyon utilized the delay to catalogue the items he must pack and the telegrams he must send.

But at the end of twenty minutes he could wait no longer; so that he left minute directions with the operator, and compounded a misdemeanor by bribing the chauffeur to break all day-time records to the Harvard Club, to his bank, and finally to the Grand Central, where he arrived, panting, at the gates just as Miss Baring emerged into the ramp in company with a porter who bore specimens of every variety of baggage except a trunk.

" I can't locate him anywhere," he said rapidly. " But there's time yet — and I don't want him to feel that we went ahead without trying our best to get him. I'll leave you at the Biltmore — you have some lunch and wait for me. Don't be scared, no matter how late I am — we can arrange everything, license and all, in half an hour!"

He deposited her in the ladies' room of the hotel, and ordered the taxicab to his apartment on Forty-fourth Street, where he prepared for Yokohama by emptying the greater part of his personal property on the floor and telling a trembling chambermaid what to pick up. In a lucid interval he telephoned the Baring office and got no satisfaction. At half past one he was back at the Biltmore, where he found Peggy placidly reading a newspaper. As he entered the room she was perusing the modern woman's page, headed " Sports," and as he hurried across to her she started and sought to confirm her eyesight by the use of an incredulous forefinger on the type.

" I can't get even so much as an idle rumor —" he began, but she stopped him.

" Harry!" she exclaimed. " Look at that!"

" We can't waste a second, dear. He's gone *somewhere* —"

" The Seniors — at Apawamis! He's entered!"

" What!" ejaculated Kenyon, seizing the paper. His eager eyes fell upon the announcement of a tournament to be inaugurated on that day, a nationally-famous handicap tournament held annually for players of fifty-five years or over; and among the entries was that of one Horatio Baring, sixty — age and handicap alike.

"He never said a *word* about it!" faltered Miss Baring. "It 's his first tournament — he never said a word!"

"The old fox!" ejaculated Kenyon. "*Now* we 'll get him!"

"If he 's *only* doing well," she prayed.

Kenyon, without replying, dashed madly to the nearby booths, and fidgeted horribly until Apawamis was on the wire.

"I want a Mr. Horatio Baring," he snapped. "He 's playing out there in the Seniors' tournament — have him come in as fast as he can make it! It 's important!"

Watch in hand, he listened restively, drumming on the desk and tapping both feet rhythmically against the partitions. After an interminable hiatus: "Not finished his first round yet?" he repeated. "Well, what of it? You can't tell what 's held him up! Why did n't you *send* for him? This is Mr. Kenyon — tell him it 's *vital!*"

Again he fretted and followed the hands of his watch to the hour of two and beyond. Mechanically he began to list the essentials of the afternoon —

264

ring, license, church, appointment with Burgess; ring, license, church, Burgess; ring, license —

"What's that?" he said, startled. *"He won't come in!* . . . Does he know who it is? . . . What was that he said? *He can't be bothered!* . . . He has n't got my message? . . . Listen! You send another boy out there as fast as he can run! . . . Tell him . . . what? Are you *sure?* . . . Well, I don't care if he's refused to take a *thousand* messages this morning — this is different! . . . You try again, and tell him it's . . . I say, tell him it's Mr. Kenyon and his daughter — he'll understand *that!* . . . Well, you forget what he said: you listen to what *I* say. . . . Don't you understand that this is *important?* . . . *Why not?* . . . Well, is n't there *some one* there who is n't afraid of losing his job? . . . All right, *get* me the manager!" . . .

The time was twenty minutes past two: in a booth at the Hotel Biltmore young Mr. Kenyon pounded the desk with his fist and wrinkled his forehead and stamped nervously and kept his ear glued to the receiver.

Far out at Apawamis, in the County of Westchester, four gray-haired gentlemen entered upon the eighteenth hole.

"All you've got to do is to keep steady, Mr.

Baring," pleaded one of them. "You 've a fighting chance yet."

"Well, that messenger boy pretty nearly got my goat," said Mr. Baring. "No wonder I took a seven — the idea of thinking they could call a man a mile back to the clubhouse in a medal round. When I 'm playing so confoundedly slow on purpose to keep steady! And I 'd *told* them not to bother me —"

He drove, in the style of Kenyon, a hundred and sixty yards on the line.

"Short, but straight, sir!"

"That 's my whole game," explained Mr. Baring, as he had explained on each of the preceding holes.

"You 're away, I think."

"Temporarily," he declared, and despatched a brassey shot a hundred and fifty yards on the line.

"A seventy net ought to win the morning prize in Class C, don't you think, Mr. Baring?"

"I need a seven for a hundred gross," said Mr. Baring frigidly. "That 'll be seventy net, but — if you don't mind — we 'll leave the bookkeeping until after the match. I never allow externals to interfere with my golf." He played a full cleek a hundred and twenty yards right on the flag.

"Four left for your seven, Mr. Baring!"

"Quite so! Stand still, caddy!" He approached neatly and went down in the standard number of putts.

"Sixty-nine net!" he exclaimed, rapturously. "*That's* not so bad! First time I ever broke a hundred, too, gentlemen!"

Around the score board a twin dozen of senior golfers jostled and pressed.

"Last foursome," intoned the marker. "All Class C? What's the net? — anything better than seventy-one? Who has the sixty-nine? Sixty-nine wins first net in Class C for the morning round!" He made the entries on the sheet: "Mr. — Horatio — Baring — of Norwood — first net — Class C! . . . The prizes are on the table in the living room."

The Class C winner, concealing his emotion with difficulty, shook hands with a number of friends and enemies masquerading as friends, and got to the living room as rapidly as he conveniently could.

On a large table were trophies, and on the trophies were placards; and that inscribed with the particular legend which most interested him hung from the handles of a silver loving cup. Mr. Baring regarded it with affection; and as he stroked the smooth surface of his prize, he thrilled with an emotion which astonished him, for he had thought that thrills were no part of his mature existence. And as he gloated over the wondrous object, an attendant touched him on the arm.

"There's some telegrams for you, Mr. Baring, and some telephone messages — after what you told the messenger we did n't disturb you again, but the parties were very angry, sir."

"Humph!" said Mr. Baring. "You should have had more sense in the first place!"

He tore open the topmost of the yellow envelopes, read the message, gulped, wet his lips, and motioned to the nearest waiter.

"A — a Scotch highball!" he managed.

He ripped the second envelope and the third, and read the long communications. One of them was dated at Harmon-on-the-Hudson, where the through trains change engines.

"No bad news, I hope?" asked his good friend and golfing opponent, Wallace.

"Peggy," said Mr. Baring hoarsely, "was married this afternoon to Harry Kenyon — they — they ran away — they —"

"Congratulations!"

"More good luck?" inquired another acquaintance, scenting greater enthusiasm than common over a simple trophy.

"Luck!" echoed Wallace. "Why, Baring's daughter's married Harry Kenyon —"

"Not *the* Kenyon? Semifinalist in the Met.?"

A dozen bystanders caught the name.

"Kenyon? Why, I know *him* — knew his father — I *do* congratulate you!"

"Good golf runs in the family, eh?"

"So *that's* where you picked up your style? I knew it was a Norwood swing —"

"You *are* in luck, Baring!"

"One of the finest young men downtown — plays just as clean a game down there as he does golf!"

"Yes, and just about as well —"

"Handicap's three, is n't it?"

To Mr. Baring's utter amazement, he was in the center of a little group which was palpably earnest and sincere in its felicitations. And now that the first shock had passed, and nothing could be done — and, after all, Kenyon was a gentleman and Mr. Baring had foreseen that sooner or later this catastrophe was bound to happen . . . besides, the loving cup was dangling in Baring's hand —

"Fill it up!" he said bruskly to a passing waiter.

"You certainly had your nerve with you on the

last few holes," complimented the man next him.
" We heard about it. That was *shooting!* "

"Oh, Baring's a wizard for a man in his first
season! "

" His first season! Why, he's a whirlwind! "

" Phenomenon! "

" Oh, rubbish! " said Mr. Baring modestly.
" I'm only beginning. But if you fellows who think
you know something about golf want to see some
real fireworks — why, once on the fourteenth hole at
Norwood, where there's a brook intended to catch
your *second* shot, I saw my son-in-law take a little
Singleton special socket brassey against the wind —"

" What happened? Who was it? " inquired a
man on the outskirts.

" *Zingo!* " said Mr. Baring expressively. " He
hit in the brook! — My son-in-law, Harry Kenyon. And, say, you ought to see that young demon
putt —"

U

DORMIE ONE

IT was five o'clock and rapidly shading into dusk. The September sun, which earlier had set the air to simmering in tremulous heat-waves, now moved reluctant to ambush behind the hills, and, as though sullen at the exigency of its time, gave warning by its bloodshot eye of pitiless heat to be renewed with to-morrow's dawn. From the curving line of trees — thin elms and maples, bordering upon the hard-packed road — long, soothing shadows edged out into the fresh green of the fairway, measuring with their deeper green the flight of hours and the peace-ful ebbing of the afternoon.

From the distant Sound, a transient breeze, shy as a maiden in the manner of its coming, ventured out from the protection of the ridge, hesitated, wavered, and passed across the sward so fleetingly that almost before it seemed assured a fact, it was a memory.

Then, from the trees at the roadside, and from the trees beyond, and from the little brook dawdling along from east to west, and from the reeded lake far over to the right, a breath of evening crept out upon the lawns, and there was silence.

In a squared clearing at the southern end of the sinuous line of maples there was a trim plateau, close-shorn of grass, and sharply defined by boundaries of sedge and stubble. From this spot forward an expansive belt of untrimmed land stretched northward for a hundred yards, to merge presently with the more aristocratic turf of the fairway. Thereafter, narrowing between the trees and a long alignment of arid pits, the trail of adventure ran through rolling country, skirted a grove of locusts, dipped down to ford the brook, climbed past a pair of shallow trenches which glistened with coarse sand, and finally found refuge on a terraced green, protected by towering chestnuts and flanked by the arm of a colonial house which rested comfortably beneath the trees.

From clearing to terrace the crow, flying as crows are popularly supposed to fly, would have accomplished five hundred and twenty yards. It was the eighteenth hole at Kenilworth.

The trim plateau, which was the eighteenth tee, now marked the apex of a human letter, a V of which a thousand men and women formed each stroke. Converging sharply toward that rectangle in the sedge, two thousand men and women — twin lines of white, slashed here and there with vivid, burning color — restrained and held in check by twisted ropes, leaned out and gaped and wondered, breathless; now standing hushed by things already seen, now vibrant to the future, uneasy, murmuring. And as in recompense for toiling through the humid afternoon, two thousand men and women held this privilege: to stand, and wait, and watch until a boy — a sturdy, laughing boy — and then a man — a grayed and quiet man — played, stroke by stroke, the eighteenth hole at Kenilworth.

And silhouetted in the background, nervous on the tee, stood man and boy, paired finalists for the Amateur Championship; two wizards of the links whose faces had gone rigid, whose palms were suddenly wet and cold, whose souls were newly strung upon the natural laws which govern flying objects. Each of them had reason for his agitation; their mutual loss of equilibrium was mutual in its cause; for of these two, the man — Hargrave, the present champion — was dormie one.

He was fifty five, this Hargrave; in commercial life he had known bankruptcy at forty. Golf, which had been heretofore diversion, he made the solace of his penury; it had then constituted itself his religion. Within a decade he had snatched the national title for his keepsake; subsequently he had lost it, struggled for it desperately, regained, and twice defended it. The gold medal meant infinitely more to him than a mere visible token of success at golf; it was suggestive of success elsewhere; it was the embodiment of conquests he had never made, of victories he never might accomplish. In other years wealth had eluded him, power had been alien to him, social distinction was to be classed among the impossibilities; but when he stepped morosely out upon the course, he vaunted in his heart that he was highborn to the purple.

Granted that he was poor indeed in purse, he knew no multimillionaire in all the world who could undertake to meet him on equal terms; he could concede six strokes, and still administer a beating, to the finest gentleman and the finest golfer in the Social Register. And so, while golf was his theology, and the arbitrary standard of par his creed, he played the Scottish game as though it symbolized the life he had proved incapable of mastering — and he mastered the game instead. It was his single virtue; it was the hyphen which allied him to the rest of civilization.

To win was the wine of his existence; to surmount obstacles was the evidence of his regeneration; to come from behind, to turn impending downfall into disconcerting triumph, was his acrid compensation for the days and months and years when the man in him had cried out for recognition, and the weakling in him had earned his failure. And he was dormie one — and it was Stoddard's honor at the last hole.

The man stiffened perceptibly as Stoddard, nodding to the referee, took a pinch of sand from the box, and teed for the final drive. Then, in accordance with the grimmest of his grim theories of golf, he abruptly turned his back on his opponent, and stared fixedly at the ground. He had trained himself to this practice for two unrelated reasons: the moral effect upon his adversary, and the opportunity to detach himself from the mechanics of his surroundings and to visualize himself in the act of playing his next stroke.

Habitually he conjured up a vision of the ball, the club, himself in the address, the swing, the attack, the aftermath. He compelled his faculties to rivet upon a superb ideal. And it was largely by virtue of this preliminary concentration that he was enabled to bring off his shots with such startling absence of delay: the orders were transmitted to his muscles in advance; his swing was often started when, to the open-mouthed observer, he had hardly reached the ball. And it was by virtue of his utter disregard of his opponent that he was never discouraged, never unnerved, never disheartened. He was neither cheered by the disaster of the enemy, nor cast down by the enemy's good fortune. He was contemptuous not only of the personality of the opponent, but also of his entity. He played his own game, and his best game, ironically ignoring the fact that it was competitive. To all intents and purposes, Hargrave in contest was the only man on the course; he even disregarded his caddy, and expected the proper club, as he demanded it, to be placed in his hand extended backwards.

But as now he formally prepared to shut Stoddard out of his consciousness, and as he exerted his stern determination to picture himself in yet another perfect illustration of golfing form, he discovered that his will, though resolute, was curiously languid. It missed of its usual persistence. The ideal came and went, as though reflected on a motion film at lowered speed. There was no continuity; there was no welding of motor impulses. According to his theory, Hargrave should have been purely mechanical. On the contrary, he was thinking.

He entertained no sense of actual antagonism toward Stoddard. Indeed, from the inception of the finals, at ten o'clock this morning, the boy had

shown himself considerate and generous, quick of
applause and slow of alibi, a dashing, brilliant,
dangerous golfer with the fire of an adventurer and
the grace of a cavalier. He was confident, yet
modest, and he had performed a score of feats for
which his modesty was none of that inverted conceit of mediocrity in luck, but literal modesty, sheer
lack of self-aggrandizement. He was dogged while
he smiled; he was still smiling with his lips when
his eyes betrayed his chastened mood; and the smile
faded and vanished only when he saw that Hargrave
was in difficulty. The gallery, nine tenths of it, was
with him boisterously. The gallery was frankly
on the side of youth and spontaneity. The mass,
unresponsive to the neutral tints of Hargrave's
character, thrilled to the juvenile star ascendant.

The gray-haired champion, introspective on the
tee, frowned and grimaced, and toyed with his
dreadnaught driver. Early in the morning he had
confessed guiltily to himself that Stoddard was the
sort of lad he should have liked to call his son.
And yet he knew that if he had ever married, if
he had ever glowed to the possession of an heir,
the boy could n't conceivably have been in the least
like Stoddard. Too many generations forbade the
miracle. The mold of ancestry would have
stamped out another failure, another charge upon

the good opinion of the world. The child would have been the father of the man. And Stoddard — witness his behavior and his generosity — was of no varnished metal. He was without alloy. He was a gentleman because his great-grandfathers had been gentlemen. He was rich because they had made him so. But Hargrave had allowed himself to experience an anomalous and paternal emotion toward Stoddard — Stoddard who at twenty was higher in rank, higher in quality, higher in the affection of the people than Hargrave at fifty five. He had nourished this emotion by trying to imagine what he could have made of himself if, at his majority, he had been of the type of Stoddard.

And now, recalling this quondam sentiment, he shuddered in a spasm of self-pity; and simultaneously, in one of those racking bursts of humanity which come to men unloving and unloved, he longed to whirl about, to stride toward Stoddard, to grip his hand and say — well, one of the common platitudes. " May the best man win "— something of that sort; anything to show that he, too, was living rapidly in the crisis.

In another moment he might have yielded; he might have bridged the fearful chasm of self-imposed restraint. But he was slothful to the impulse.

Behind him there was the sharp, pistol-like crack
of a clean and powerful drive; and before him,
brought clear by reflex and by the will that had
been lagging, the ghostly mirage of a ball, and of
himself swinging steadily and hard, and of the joy
of impact, and a tremendous carry and run, true to
the flag. The champion had remembered that he
was dormie one. A voice, low but distinct, came
to him through a volume of incoherent sound:
" Mr. Hargrave! "

The man turned slowly. He saw neither the
referee, who had spoken to him, nor Stoddard, who
had stepped aside; he saw no caddies; he saw no
fairway. Both lines of the V were weaving, undulating; on the faces of the men and women nearest
him he perceived beatific, partizan delight. The
thousand-tongued shout which had gone up in praise
of Stoddard was dwindling by degrees to a pleasant
hum, which throbbed mercilessly in Hargrave's ears
and challenged him. He knew, as he had known
for hours, how earnestly the public hoped for his
defeat. He knew that if he bettered Stoddard's
drive his sole reward would be a trifling ripple of
applause, smirched by a universal prayer that
ineptly he might spoil his second shot.

He grinned sardonically at the throng. He
rubbed his palms together, drying them. He teed

a ball, and took his stance; glanced down the course, took back the club a dozen inches, carried it ahead, and rested for the fraction of a second; then, accurate, machine-like to the tiniest detail, swung up, hit down, and felt his body carried foward in the full, strong finish of a master drive.

"Good ball!" said Stoddard in a voice that trembled slightly. From the V — sporadic hand-clapping. Hargrave, the national champion, had driven two hundred and sixty yards.

Ahead of him, as he walked defiantly through the rough, the fairway bobbed with men and women who, as they chattered busily, stumbled over the irregularities of the turf. Now and then a straggler threw a look of admiration over his shoulder, and, meeting the expressionless mask of the amateur champion, insouciantly shrugged that shoulder and resumed his march.

Hargrave's caddy, dour and uncommunicative as the champion himself, stalked abreast, the clubs rattling synchronously to his stride. Hargrave was studying the contour of the land in front; he glowered at the marshals who had suffered the gallery to break formation and overflow the course; and he was tempted to ask his caddy how, when the entire middle distance was blocked by gabbling spectators, the Golf Association thought a finalist could judge the hole. But he denied himself the question; it was seven years since he had condescended to complain of, or to criticize, the conditions of any tournament. Nevertheless he was annoyed; he was certain that the ground sloped off just where his second shot should properly be placed; his memory was positive. Blindfold, he could have aimed correctly to a surveyor's minute.

Still, he was impatient, irritated. He wanted to verify his scheme of play. He wanted to do it instantly. The muscles of his neck twitched spasmodically; and without warning, even to himself, his canker flared into red hate. His eyes flashed venomously; and when it seemed that unless that crowd dispersed, and gave him room, his nerves would shatter in a burst of rage, he saw the marshals tautening their lines, the gallery billowing out into a wide and spacious funnel, and felt the caddy's timid touch upon his sleeve.

"Look out, Mr. Hargrave! Stoddard's away!"

The champion halted, and without a glance toward Stoddard, stared at his own ball. It was an excellent lie; he nodded imperceptibly and took a brassey which the caddy, without instructions, placed in his outstretched hand. His fingers closed around the smooth-worn grip; he tested the spring of the shaft, and focused his whole attention upon the ball. He strove to summon that mental cinema of Hargrave, cool, collected, playing a full brassey to the green. But Stoddard again intruded.

In the morning round, Hargrave had won the first three holes in a row, and he had held the advantage, and brought in his man three down. He had made a seventy-four, one over par, and Stoddard had scored a creditable seventy-eight — doubly creditable in view of his ragged getaway. And in the afternoon Hargrave had won the first two holes, and stood five up with sixteen more to play, when Stoddard had begun an unexpected spurt. Hargrave scowled at the toe of his brassey as he recounted errors which, if they could have been eliminated from his total, would have erased five needless strokes, and ended the match long since. Cruelly, three of those errors were on successive holes. On the fifteenth he had missed a simple putt for the win; on the sixteenth he had overapproached and thrown away a half; on the seventeenth he had topped an iron and still accomplished a par four — but Stoddard had made a three.

The champion felt his heart flutter and his knees yield a trifle as he reflected what havoc one more ineffectual shot would work upon his nerves. He was surely, steadily slipping, and he knew it. The bulk of his vitality was gone; and he was drawing heavily upon his light reserve. He realized, not in cowardice but in truth and in fact, that if the match should go to an extra hole, he, and not Stoddard, would be the loser. His customary command of his muscles was satisfactory, but his control of his nerves was waning. He was overgolfed; overstrained; stale. He could bear the strain of this hole, but that was all. His stamina had touched its limit; his fortitude could stand no more. He could gage it to a nicety; he had a debilitating intuition which told him that if he had to drive again from the first tee, he should founder wretchedly; and he believed this message from his soul, because he had never before received it.

If Stoddard won the eighteenth, it would be the fourth consecutive godsend for Stoddard, and Stoddard's game was improving, not deteriorating; he had moral courage behind him, he had the savage exhilaration of metamorphosing a forlorn chance into a delirious certainty, he had the stimulus and the impetus of his grand onrush, he had the responsive gallery to cheer him on. It was inevitable that Stoddard, if he won the eighteenth, would win the next; so that the champion, who was dormie one, must have a half — he must divide this hole with Stoddard. He *must!*

The champion grew restive. It needed the supreme effort of his career to force himself to inertia,
to refrain from wheeling swiftly, and shrieking
aloud to Stoddard, to demand why he did n't *play!*
Was the boy asleep? Dead? Dreaming? Had
he succumbed to paralysis? Was he gloating over
his triumph? Hargrave wet his lips, and swallowed
dustily.

A tremor ran through his limbs, and his wrists
tightened in palsied fear. His eyes pained him;
they reminded him of a doll's eyes, turning inward;
he was aware that his face was drawn. He wondered stupidly whether the spoon would be safer
than the brassey. He liked the spoon — but was
the cleek surer yet? He caught his breath in a gasp,
and at the same moment his spine was chilled in a
paroxysm of futile terror. He essayed once more
to swallow and thought that he was strangling. His
soul cried heart-breakingly out to Stoddard:
" Shoot! For God's sake, *shoot!* "

The tension snapped. A roar of jubilance went
up from twice a thousand throats, a roar which,
dying momentarily, swelled up in glory, and hung,
and splintered into a thousand reverberations against
the hills. Hargrave shivered and cleared his
throat. For the life of him he could n't maintain

his principles; his nature revolted; and jerking his head towards the north, he was gazing at a tiny fleck of white ten feet to the side of the terrace, which was the eighteenth green. Stoddard was hole high in two! A lucky ricochet from the stones of the brook! Five hundred and twenty yards in two! Hargrave went sickly white, and looked despairingly at his caddy.

He needed a half, and Stoddard was hole high. There was an outside possibility, then, that Stoddard could make a four — one under par. And Hargrave was nearly three hundred yards away. Could he, too, make a four — for the half?

The champion, with two alternatives looming bold before him, shuddered in exquisite incertitude. He could attempt a heroic stroke with the brassey, sacrificing accuracy for distance, or he could play his normal shot, which was practically sure to clear the brook, but still would leave him at a critical disadvantage. In the latter instance he could guarantee himself a five, but already Stoddard was assured of four. And that four, if he achieved it, meant a squared match for Stoddard, and a resultant victory. Hargrave could halve the hole only if Stoddard blundered; and for an hour and more Stoddard's golf had been flawless. There was no blunder in him.

DORMIE ONE

But if Hargrave should risk his own crown on a mighty endeavor to equal Stoddard's titanic brassey shot, he would have the odds of war alarmingly against him. The trajectory must be perfect to a ruled, undeviating line. The ball must either fall short of the brook by ten yards, or clear it by ten, and bounding neither to the left, among the trees, nor to the right, among the sand-pits, surmount the grade. An unfortunate angle of consequence, a mere rub of the green, would be doubly fatal. The ball might even be unplayable. There would yet be a hazardous last chance for a five; but again, there was no reason to expect that Stoddard would need so many. Stoddard had been deadly, uncannily deadly, on those short, running approaches. Stoddard would make his four, and Hargrave knew it. He closed and unclosed his fingers around the grip of his brassey. A rim of ice, pressing inward, surrounded his heart. His brain was delicately clouded, as though he had just awakened out of the slumber of exhaustion, and looked upon the world without comprehending it, sensed it without perceiving its physiology. He passed a hand over his forehead, and found it damp with perspiration.

A year ago he had promised himself that, as cham-

pion, he would withdraw from competition. It
was his dream to retire at the height of his prowess,
to go down in the history of games as one of that
rare company who have known when to file their
resignations. Indeed, as late as February he had
vowed not to defend his title this year. But when
he had once sniffed the intoxicant atmosphere of a
club grill, and after he had proved his strength in
a practice round or two, he had diffidently entered
for the Atlantic City tournament, and won it. In-
fectiously, the old ardor had throbbed in his veins.
He was keenly alive to his dominant tenure; his
nostrils dilated, his jaws set.

He would add one consummating honor to those
that had gone before; he would take his third successive championship with him into exile. And so
at Deal, at Apawamis, at Sleepy Hollow and at
Garden City, at Montclair and Wykagyl and Piping
Rock, he had groomed himself, thoroughly and deliberately, for the fitting climax. The metropolitan
supremacy was his for the fifth occasion; he had
finished fourth in the Metropolitan Open, third in
the National Open. In the handicap list of the
great central association he stood proudly aloof at
scratch. He was invincible.

And now, with six days of irreproachable golf behind him; with the greatest prize of a lifetime shin-

ing in his very eyes, he looked at a distant red flag,
drooping on its staff, and looked at a ball lying in
tempting prominence on the fairway, and felt his
chin quiver in the excess of his passionate longing,
and felt a white-hot band searing his forehead, and
penetrating deep.

He kept the brassey. And as he took his stance,
and struggled to centralize his wishes upon the problem of combining vast length with absolute precision,
his mind became so acutely receptive to impression,
so marvelously subjective, that he found himself re-
peating over and over to himself the series of simple maxims he had learned painfully by heart when
he was a novice, striving to break through the dread
barrier which divides those who play over and those
who play under a hundred strokes for the single
round.

He experienced, for the first time in years, a sub-
tle premonition of ineptitude. He was again a tyro,
whose margin of error was ninety-five per cent.
Where was the ball going? It was incredibly small,
that sphere in the fairway; it was incredible that he
should smite it so truly and so forcibly that it would
fly even so far as a welcome furlong. Suppose he,
a champion, with a champion's record, should slice,
or pull, or top — or miss the ball completely?

Hargrave's teeth came grindingly together. His

eyes dulled and contracted. He took the club back
for a scant foot, raised it, took it forward, past the
ball in the line of the hole, brought it to its original
position, pressed it gently into the velvet turf with
infinitesimal exertion of the left wrist, and swung.
Wrists, forearms, shoulders and hips — his whole
anatomy coördinated in that terrible assault. The
click of the wood against the ball had n't yet reached
his ears when he knew, with exultation so stupen-
dous that it nauseated him, that the shot had come
off. His eager eyes picked up the ball in flight; and
as he paused momentarily at the finish of his terrific
drive, he was filled with a soft and yet an incon-
gruously fierce content. Again he had foiled the
gallery, and Stoddard! He saw the ball drop,
across the brook; saw it leap prodigiously high in
air, and fall again, and bound, and roll, slower and
slower, and cease to roll — a good club's length
from the lower pit, twenty yards from the green.

The champion and the challenger were on even
terms.

Unlike the average man of gregarious instincts,
Hargrave never sought proximity to his opponent
during a match. His procedure was exactly as
though, instead of playing against a flesh-and-blood
antagonist, he were going around alone. He went

his independent way, kept his peace, and entertained
no thought of conversation or courtesy. If fortu-
itously he had to walk a course parallel to that of
his opponent, and even if the interval between them
were a matter of a scant rod or so, the champion
was invariably thin-lipped, reflective, incommunica-
tive.

He observed with a little flicker of amusement,
that Stoddard was eying him sidewise, and he felt
that Stoddard was not a little affected by that enormous brassey, as well as by Hargrave's outward indifference toward it. Hargrave, however, appraised
his own flinty exterior as one of his championship
assets. He never praised the other man; and if the
other man chose to burst into fervid eulogy, the
champion's manner was so arctic, so repelling, that
not infrequently he gained a point on the very next
shot through the adversary's dazed inefficiency and
even one stroke in match play is worth saving.

He knew that he was unpopular, he knew that he
was affirmatively disliked; he knew that the public,
the good-natured and friendly public, yearned for
Stoddard's triumph rather as a vindication of gentility than as a proof of might. But as he observed
that Stoddard showed premonitory symptoms of increased nervousness, and that Stoddard was impelled to speak, and yet held his tongue to save him-

self from sure rebuff, the champion's breast expanded with golden hope.

Stoddard, after all, was a mere boy: a veteran golfer — yes, but immature in the mentality of golf. And Hargrave sometimes won his matches, especially from younger men, in the locker-room before he put on his shoes. If Stoddard congratulated him now, he could send Stoddard into catastrophe with one glowing sentence. But Stoddard did n't speak.

In addition to his other reasons, he was anxious to beat Stoddard because of his very youth. It had galled Hargrave to be called, by the luck of the draw, to meet five of the youngest experts of the country in this tournament; it had galled him, not ' because he was loath to win from younger men, but because the public naturally discounted his victories over them.

On Tuesday he had overwhelmed a Western prodigy, a freckled schoolboy who had blushingly donned full-length trousers for this great event. On Wednesday he had won, three up and two to go, from a Harvard freshman, a clubbable youngster who had capitulated to Hargrave primarily because his optimism had slowly been destroyed by Hargrave's rude acerbity. On Thursday he had met, and easily defeated, the junior champion of

Westchester — defeated him by the psychology of
the locker-room, by knocking him off balance at the
outset, much as the gladiator Corbett once shook the
poise of the gladiator Sullivan. In the semi-finals
yesterday he had beaten his man — browbeaten him
— by diligently creating an atmosphere of such electric stress that a too-little-hardened Southron, sensitive as a girl, had gone to pieces at the ninth, surrendered at the twenty-seventh hole.

And Hargrave, whose bitterness toward the golfing world had progressed arithmetically through
these earlier rounds, had come up to the finals in
a mood of acid which, in the true analysis, was a
form of specious envy and regret. He realized
that in comparison with any of the men he had removed from brackets, he was unattractive, aged,
cynical, repugnant. He envied youth — but how
could he regain his own? How could he crystallize
at fifty-five the secret ambitions of a boy too young
to vote? He could n't stand before this fashionable
gallery and, indicating Stoddard, cry out to them:
" But I *want* to be like him! I *want* to be! And
it 's too late! It 's too late! "

A great wave of self-glorification swept over him,
and left him calmer, more pragmatical. After all,
he was Hargrave, phenomenon of the links, the man

who, beginning serious golf at the age of forty, un-aided by professional tutoring, unschooled by previ-ous experience in the realm of sport, had wrenched three amateur championships and unnumbered lesser prizes from keen fields. He was the unconquerable Hargrave; the man who had victoriously invaded France, England, Austria, Canada, Scotland. He had averaged below seventy-five for the previous three years on all courses and at all seasons. He had been six down with nine to play in the finals of the English Amateur, and come romping home to triumph, four under par. It was said of him that he was never beaten until the last putt on the last hole. Better than that, it was true.

By this time the gallery was massed rows deep around the eighteenth green. Hargrave crossed the little footbridge over the brook and permitted the vestige of a smile to temper the severity of his face. They hoped to see him lose, did they? Well, he had often disappointed them in the past; he could disappoint them now! All he required was a half, and he was barely off the green in two.

But even in the vanity which somewhat relieved the strain upon him, he was conscious of a burden-ing weariness which was n't solely physical. He was impatient, not only to end the hole, and the match, but also to end his tournament golf forever.

He was sure now that, winner or loser, he should never enter an important contest again. His nerves were disintegrating. He was losing that essential balance without which no man, however skilful in the academics of the game, may be renowned for his examples.

Next year he should unquestionably play with less surety, less vigor. Some unknown duffer would catch him unawares and vanquish him; and after that the descent from scratch would be rapid — headlong. It had been so with the greatest golfers of old; it would be so with Hargrave. Great as he was, he was n't immune to the calendar. But to retire as merely a runner-up — that was unthinkable! To retire in favor of a slim boy whose Bachelorhood of Arts was yet a fond delusion — that was impossible! He *must* win — and on the eighteenth green, after he had holed out, he would break his putter over his knee, and he would say to the gallery — and it ought to be dramatic. . . .

He brought himself to a standstill. His heart pounded suffocatingly. A lump rose in his throat, and choked him, and his whole intellect seemed to melt into confusion and feeble horror; there was a crushing weight on his chest. A slow, insistent cacophony poured through his brain, and for an instant his universe went black. The ball, which had appeared to carry so magnificently, and roll so well, and found a bowl-shaped depression in the turf, a wicked concavity an inch and a half in depth, two in diameter; and there it lay, part in the sunlight, part nestling under the shelter of a dry leaf, a ball accursed and sinister.

Blindly, and apprehensive, the champion turned to look at Stoddard. The boy was struggling to conceal the manifestation of his hopes; the muscles of his lower face were flexed and unrelenting. Between him and the flag was level turf, untroubled by the slightest taint of trickery or unevenness. He knew, and Hargrave knew, that nothing short of superhuman skill could bring the like to Hargrave. He knew, and Hargrave knew, that at the play-off of a tie the champion was doomed. The champion had faltered on the last few holes; his game was destined to collapse as surely as Stoddard's game was destined to rise supreme. As Hargrave paused, aghast, there came a rustle and a murmur from the gallery. A clear voice — a woman's voice — said ecstatically, " Then Bobby 'll *win* — won't he? "

Hargrave glared in the direction of that voice. The veil of horror had gradually dissolved, but Hargrave, as he weighed the enigma of the shot, was visited by a cold apathy which staggered him.

It was n't a phlegmatic calm which sat upon him; it was inappetency — as though he had just been roused to a sense of proportionate values.

The matter of coaxing a golf ball out of a casual depression — what significance had it? To-morrow would yet be to-morrow; with breakfast, and the newspapers, and all the immaterial details of living and breathing. Why all this pother and heartache about it? What was golf, that it should stir a man to the otherwise unprobed depths of his soul? Why should he care, why should he squander so much mental torture as could be computed by one tick of a clock, why should he tremble at this ridiculous experiment with a little white ball and a bit of iron on the end of a shaft of hickory?

For one elemental moment he was almost irresistibly impelled to pick that ball out of its lie, and dash it in the face of the gallery, hurl his clubs after it, and empty himself of the accumulated passion of fifty-five years. Sulphurous phrases crowded to his lips. . . .

And then he realized that all this time he had been glaring in the direction of a woman's voice. He exhaled fully, and held his hand out backwards to the caddy.

" Niblick! " said Hargrave thickly.

The distance to the hole was greater than he had fancied. The lie of the ball was worse than he had feared. His calculation intimated that he must strike hard, and stiffly, with a pronounced up-and-down swing to get at the back of the ball. The force of the extricating stroke must be considerable; the green, however, was too fast, too fine, to permit liberty in the manner of approaching it. The ball, if it were to carry the full thirty yards to the pin, couldn't possibly receive sufficient reverse power to fall dead. It must, therefore, be played to reach the nearer rim of the green, and to drift gently on to the hole.

Hargrave caught his breath. The knowledge that he distrusted himself was infinitely more demoralizing than any other factor in the personal equation; he was shocked and baffled by his own uncertainty. Through his brain ran unceasingly the first tenets of the kindergarten of golf. He didn't imagine himself playing this shot: he speculated as to how Braid, or Vardon, or Ray or Duncan would play it. He was strangely convinced that for any one else on earth it would be the simplest of recoveries, the easiest of pitches to the green.

He glanced at his caddy, and in that glance there was hidden an appeal which bespoke genuine pathos. Hargrave wasn't merely disturbed and distressed:

he was palpitatingly afraid. He was afraid to strike, and he was afraid not to strike. His mind had lost its jurisdictive functions; he felt that his thews and sinews were in process of revolt against his will. He was excruciatingly perceptive of people watching him; of Stoddard regarding him humorously.

The collective enmity of the gallery oppressed and befuddled him. He was crazily in dread that when he swung the niblick upright, some one would snatch at it and divert its orbit. His ears strained for a crashing sound from the void; his overloaded nerves expected thunder. He knew that the fall of an oak-leaf would reverberate through his aching head like an explosion of maximite and make him strike awry. His vitals seemed suddenly to slip away from his body, leaving merely a febrile husk of clammy skin to hold his heart-beats. The throbbing of the veins in his wrists was agony.

The niblick turned in his perspiring hands. He gripped more firmly, and as his wrists reacted to the weight of the club-head, he was automatic. The niblick rose, and descended, smashing down the hinder edge of the bowl-like cavity, and tearing the ball free. A spray of dust sprang up, and bits of sod and dirt. The ball shot forward, overrunning the hole by a dozen feet. Almost before it

came to rest, Stoddard played carefully with a jigger, and landed ten inches from the hole.

Hargrave's sensation was that he was encompassed with walls which were closing in to stifle and crush him. That they were living walls was evident by the continuous whisper of respiration, and by the cross-motion of the sides. He was buried under the tremendous weight of thousands of personalities in conflict with his own. He tottered on the verge of hysteria. He was nervously exhausted, and yet he was upheld, and compelled to go on, to play, to putt, by nervous energy which by its very goad was unendurable. Hargrave looked at the green under his feet, and fought back a mad impulse to throw himself prone upon it, to scream at the top of his lungs, and writhe, to curse and blaspheme, and claw the grass with his nails. Each breath he drew was cousin to a sob.

He stood behind the ball to trace the line, and recognized that he was seeing neither the ball nor the hole. He could n't see clearly the grass itself. He was stricken, as far as his environment was concerned, with utter ophthalmia. And although the boy Stoddard was outside the scope of Hargrave's vision, the champion saw Stoddard's face, as he had seen it just now, before Stoddard turned away.

He despised Stoddard; unreasonably but implacably
he despised him, because of the light he had seen
in Stoddard's eyes. The boy was n't a philosopher,
like Hargrave: he was a baby, a whining infant
grasping for the moon. *He* had no sense of pro-
portion. That expression in his eyes had con-
victed him. This tournament was to him the horizon of his life. It *was* his life!

Hargrave's mouth was parched and bitter. He
tried to moisten his lips. Details of the green began to develop in his consciousness as in a photo-
graphic negative. He saw the zinc-lined hole
twelve feet away. His eye traced an imaginary
line, starting from his ball and leading, not straight
to the cup, but perceptibly to the left, then curving
in along the briefest of undulations, swerving past
a tiny spot where the grass was sun-scorched, and
so to the haven of the hole.

If he could sink that curling putt, nothing could
deprive him of his victory. He would be down in
four, and Stoddard now lay three. He would have
a half — and the match by one up in thirty-six
holes. He would be the Amateur Champion of the
United States — and he could quit! He could quit
as the only man who ever won in three successive
years. And if he missed, and Stoddard took the

hole in four to five, Hargrave knew that even if his legs would support him to the first tee, his arms would fall at the next trial. He doubted if sanity itself would stay with him for another hole.

The murmur of the gallery appalled him with its vehemence. The noice was as the rushing of the falls of Niagara. Hargrave stood wearily erect, and eyed that section of the crowd which was before him. He was puzzled by the excitement, the anxiety of that crowd. He was violently angered that no smile of encouragement, of good-fellowship, met his inquiring gaze. The misanthrope in him surged to the surface, and he was supercilious — just for a second! — and then that sense of impotence, of futility, of shaken poise fell upon him once more, and his throat filled.

He needed the half. He must hole this putt. He was thinking now not so much of the result of holding it as of the result of missing it. He could fancy the wretched spectacle he would make of himself on the play-off; he could fancy the explosive, tumultuous joy of the gallery; he could picture the dumb, stunned radiance of Stoddard. And Stoddard was so young. Hargrave would n't have minded defeat at the hands of an older man, he told himself fiercely — but at the hands of a boy! Hargrave, the man who had made more whirlwind finishes than any other two players of the game, beaten by a stripling who had come from behind!

On the sixteenth and seventeenth holes the champion had reviled himself, scourged himself, between shots. He had clenched his teeth and sworn to achieve perfection. He had persuaded himself that each of his mishaps had been due to carelessness; and he had known in his heart that each of them was due to a fault, a palpable fault of execution. On the eighteenth hole he had reverted to sincerity with himself. He was harrowed and upset, and in confessing his culpability he had removed at least the crime of over-confidence. But this was far worse! He was doubting his own judgment now: he had determined upon the line of his putt, and he was reconsidering it.

He peered again and, blinking, discovered that there were tears in his eyes. The hole seemed farther away than ever, the green less true, the bare spot more prominent, the cup smaller. He wondered dully if he had n't better putt straight for the hole. He braced himself, and tremblingly addressed the ball with his putter. This was the shot that would take stomach! This was the end!

He had a vision of to-morrow, and the day after, and the day after that. If he missed this putt, and lost the match, how could he exonerate himself? He had no other pleasure in life, he had no other recreation, no other balm for his wasted years. If he tried again next season, he would lose in the first round. He knew it. And he might live to be seventy — or eighty — always with this gloomy pall of failure hanging over him. Another failure — another Waterloo! And this time he would be to himself the apotheosis of failure! Why — Hargrave's heart stopped beating — *he would n't be champion!*

With a final hum, which was somehow different from those that had preceded it, the gallery faded from his consciousness. Stoddard was as though he had never existed. Hargrave bent over the putter, and a curious echo rang not unpleasantly in his ears. He saw a white ball in the sunlight, a stretch of lawn, a zinc-lined hole in shadow. There was no longer an objective world in which he lived; there were no longer men and women. He himself was not corporeal. His brain, his rationality, were lost in the abysmal gulf of nothingness. He was merely a part of geometric space; he was an atom of that hypothetical line between two points. His whole being was, for the moment, the essence of the linear standard.

In a blank detachment — for he had no recollection of having putted — he saw the ball spinning on a course to the left of the hole. A terrible agony seized him, and for the second time a black curtain shut him off from actuality. It lifted, leaving him on the brink of apoplexy, and he saw that the ball had curved correctly to the fraction of an inch, and was just dropping solidly and unerringly into the cup.

And from the morning paper:

Hargrave was dormie one. Both men drove two hundred and fifty yards straight down the course. Stoddard banged away with his brassey, and nearly got home when the ball caromed off a stone in the brook. Hargrave, playing with that marvelous rapidity which characterizes his game, would n't be downed, and promptly sent off a screaming brassey which found a bad lie just off the green, but after studying it fully ten seconds — twice his usual allowance — he chipped out prettily with a niblick. Stoddard ran up, dead. Hardly glancing at the line of his fifteen-footer, Hargrave confidently ran down the putt for a birdie four, and the match. Probably no man living would have played the hole under similar conditions, with such absence of nerves and such abnormal assurance. From tee to green Hargrave barely addressed the ball at all. And certainly in the United States, if not in the world, there is no player who can compete with Hargrave when the champion happens to be in a fighting mood.

To our reporter Hargrave stated positively after the match that he will defend his title next year.

" CONSOLATION "

WITHOUT prejudice, it was the gown which first attracted Meredith's attention. It was the simplest of all possible gowns, a black-velvet reminiscence of an old daguerreotype, drooping delicately from the shoulders in short, puffed sleeves; it had a trim, pointed little bodice, and a gently flaring little skirt, and not one woman in a thousand would have remembered to wear it without jewelry and to avoid any artificial contrast of color. The girl who was dancing in it, however, was an artist; she had n't even stooped to the banality of a red rose for her corsage, and she had done her hair to suit the period of her costume. She was so pretty that Meredith, after enjoying the sheer luxury of staring at her, refused to rest until he had unearthed a friend who could present him; she was so ineffably sweet and lovable that after he had met her and talked with her and danced with her to the swing of " Poor Butterfly," which was the prime obsession of that Pinehurst season, he could hardly credit the obvious reality that they were both alive and abiding. This was in December, and by the

307

middle of the following month he was head over heels in love with her. The delay was chiefly due to the fact that, unless it rained, he saw Miss Winsted only during the evenings and on Sundays.

In the meantime he had gone resolutely about his serious business in Pinehurst, which was to compensate himself for a four-years' hiatus in his golfing career and to renew his quondam skill at the game to which he was passionately devoted. He had two objectives, the St. Valentine's and the Spring tournaments, and he went about his self-schooling for them as though his life depended on the outcome. For three hours every morning he had practised diligently, beginning with two-foot putts, and working methodically backward to jigger, iron, cleek, spoon, and driver. Thirty minutes of each forenoon he had spent doggedly in sand traps, seeking now for distance, now for accuracy on short clips to a neighboring green, now for simple outs from difficult lies. After lunch he had played a painstaking round alone, preferably over the No. 2 course, with its hundred and ninety ambushed hazards, and had struggled religiously to erase from his mind any record of his medal score. He did n't want to be elated or distressed by his performances; he wanted to bring about a logical development of his game until it approximated his undergraduate standard. He was interested in the present only as a stepping-stone to the future. Not oftener than twice a week he had played against a flesh-and-blood opponent, and on the next day he had revisited the same course, and practised faithfully all those shots on which he had made mistakes. The result of this sound preparation was that Meredith, without achieving any notoriety, was habitually around eighty on his solitary rounds; but partly because he had so relentlessly effaced himself, and partly because his collegiate reputation had n't preceded him to the Carolinas, he was still registered at the club-house in Class B, which, being interpreted according to the equable Pinehurst system, required him to qualify not lower than the second flight in any tournament or be disfranchised. Not having a national rating, and not having played in previous events at Pinehurst, he was n't eligible to Class A, which would have compelled him to make the first division or to withdraw; and this pleased him inordinately, because he knew that when he came to match-play his partners would expect Class B golf from him, and would n't get it.

He was bitterly disappointed to discover that Miss Winsted, although she rode and swam and played tennis, and spent the majority of her waking hours out of doors, did n't comprehend even the terminology of golf. Furthermore, she displayed a mild but lively antipathy to it. Golf, she said, might be a very nice game,— indeed, it probably was,— but she herself liked the more active sports. She had observed that whenever you scratch a golfer, you find a chatterbox, and she could n't understand why people should talk all night to explain why they had played badly all day. When an afternoon of tennis was over, it was over; when the hounds had caught the fox, every one but the fox was satisfied, and in the evening there was either dancing or bridge. Meredith, of course, was an exception, and she admired him for his versatility of conversation; but even in his case she could n't promote a thrill at his report of a miraculous recovery from the Bermuda grass, and his story of a three on the tenth hole left her as unmoved as though he had merely purled two and knitted two, and thrown off the neck. Still, despite the vital defect, he fell in love with her, and this proves that she was superlative.

On the day before the qualifying round for the St. Valentine's he had gone out at half-past seven in the morning for his final grooming, and when next his spikes next bit the floor of the locker-room he was inwardly radiant. On this, his last trial, he had achieved a sterling seventy-four; his long game

had been adequate, his approaching and putting almost professional.   There was nothing left for him
to do; he must stand or fall on the quality of his
game as he had established it.   Buoyantly he put
away his clubs; then, because he was mindful of the
principles of training, he determined to remove himself as far as possible from the links.   He would
refresh himself spiritually as well as physically.
He would rest for the afternoon, and tee off to-morrow with no handicap of nerves or staleness.   So he
quitted the club-house without lingering to analyze
his score, and walked back toward the hotel; and
when on the way he encountered Miss Winsted
feeding loaf-sugar to the fawns in the tiny deer inclosure, he realized at once that the meeting was
providential.

"*Good* morning," he said cheerfully.   "Well,
it 's on the knees of the gods."

"What is?" she inquired with equal cheer.   She
was probably the only girl in all Pinehurst who
did n't know who were the favorites in the pool on
the first sixteen, and *she* hardly knew there was
a competition!

"The St. Valentine's Tournament," explained
Meredith.   "Starts to-morrow — two hundred and
fifty entries."

"Oh."   Miss Winsted had apparently expected

something more important. " Are you playing in it ? "

Meredith could n't check an involuntary smile.

" Rather ! " he said. " It 's what you might call epochal for me. I 've been looking forward to it for two solid years. Think of it, until last month I had n't had a club in my hands since the inter-collegiates in 1912! And all that time, when I was too busy to play, I planned for this and dreamed of it and saved up my vacation for it; and now I 'm here! It 's almost too good to be true."

Miss Winsted dispensed the few remaining cubes of sugar, and dusted her palms neatly.

" You do seem awfully happy about it," she commented.

" It 's a curious game," said Meredith. " It 's the most curious game there is. My idea of a pure vacation is to play golf, and yet I 'm doubly joyful to-day because I 'm not going around again this afternoon: it 's a respite within a respite. Why can't we do something together? "

She regarded him half humorously, and her intonation was bantering.

" You don't mean," she said, " that you 'd sacrifice golf for a *girl* — on a day like this! "

" No sacrifice at all," denied Meredith. " I 'm at liberty for nearly twenty-four hours. So if there 's anything you'd especially like to do, and if you are n't tied up to a party, and if there are n't too many other ifs, why, I do wish we could fix it up somehow."

"I'll tell you," said Miss Winsted. "I've an appointment at eleven, but you come and lunch at our table, and we'll talk it over. Will you?"

The upshot of it was that they went riding, and that Meredith presently found himself expounding his ideals, a danger-signal which Miss Winsted chose to disregard. Vastly heartened by her manner, Meredith ventured to touch upon his age and his income. And somewhat later, when the geography of the ride was favorable, he abruptly told her that he wanted her and needed her. He admitted that he did n't deserve her, and yet, by the usual boyish implication, he invited her to dispute him. When he had quite finished, he reined close to her and put his arm around her and kissed her awkwardly; and, to his amazed beatitude, she looked at him with soft and shining eyes and confessed that she was glad. When they eventually reappeared at the hotel they were engaged, and Meredith had conceived an idyl which, to any woman who played golf, would have appealed tremendously.

He did n't endow her with the romance until after dinner. Then, when they had shyly separated themselves from the merry circle in the lobby, and assured each other that they had kept their vows of secrecy except for letters to their immediate families, he escorted her to the corner where stood a huge table loaded with heavy silverware.

" Dearest," said Meredith under his breath, " if you played golf yourself, you 'd know what this means to me. For four years I 've *suffered* — and now I 've got it back again, and got you, too! And there are a lot of men in Pinehurst to play for this trophy; but I 'm going better and better, and next Saturday I 'm going to give it to you — for an engagement present!" He indicated a massive platter built on the lines of a terrace. " That 's for the championship!" His expression was seraphic; he could translate now the motives underlying the ancient courts of chivalry, and although the killing of Saracens has gone out of fashion as a pledge of affection, her first pride in him should nevertheless be for a famous conquest.

Miss Winsted glanced apprehensively at him and at the platter. The magnificence of it, and its extravagance of etching, frankly appalled her. She strongly approved his zeal to win a memento for her, but her tastes in decorative silverware were highly conservative. She hesitated, and finally put her forefinger upon a small card-tray, plain and unadorned save for the Pinehurst crest and a line or two of script engraving.

" I 'd much rather have that one," she told him, flushing.

Meredith was startled, but he respected her ingenuousness, and spoke with great courtesy.

" But, my dear, the big one is the President's trophy ! "

Miss Winsted was utterly unimpressed.

" You could n't very well give me a steak-platter for an engagement present," she said, with a ripple of laughter. " Why, Dicky ! But I 'd *love* to have you win that little tray for me. It 's so nice and repressed. And everything else there is here is just blatant."

" That little tray," said Meredith, examining it indulgently, " is for the runner-up of the second flight."

" You win it for me," she begged him. " I 'd be so proud to have you — in a game you like so much."

Although he had n't by any means lost his sense of humor, Meredith was beginning to be vaguely troubled. Miss Winsted was so positive, so unyielding in her innocence. There was something almost pathetic in her deprecation of glory and her predilection for the chaste little tray, and he adored her for it; but he had been a golfer long before he became a fiancé.

"I'm sorry, dear," he said kindly, "but I have to play for the other one, you know. It isn't exactly ethical to go out for anything but the best."

Miss Winsted, whose ignorance of golf was colossal, lifted her face to his. Her whole bearing was that of a pleader not subject to overruling.

"You'll let me pick out my own engagement present, won't you, Dicky?" Her voice was subtly freighted with astonishment that she had been compelled to ask twice.

Meredith was increasingly thoughtful.

"Eleanor," he said, with reassuring tenderness, "you don't understand. Why, I'd rather not play in the tournament at all than to win the runner-up prize in the second flight. You see —" He stopped short at the reaction which showed in her eyes. For a matter of hours they had been engaged, and already he had hurt her. She wasn't cognizant of golfing morals; she didn't fully grasp Meredith's overwhelming infatuation for golf; all she knew was that here were prizes, and that specifically she wanted one of them and no other. Palpably, she thought that he was unreasonable and perhaps a trifle stubborn.

"But I *want* you to play," she insisted. "I just

want you to win me something for a remembrance. Can't you play for whatever prize you like?"

" Not exactly," said Meredith. " Of course it 's humanly possible to try to win any definite trophy, but —"

" Then I want the card-tray," said Miss Winsted, firmly. " I 'm crazy about it, and I 'll be *so* proud of you —"

" My dear girl, I 'm afraid I can't —"

" Can't?" she puzzled. " I thought you were a good player."

" I know; but the point is that I 've been working for this tournament for weeks. I 've looked forward to it for years. I'm going pretty well, and —"

" But don't you *see?* I want you to play, Dicky; of course I do! But would n't you rather give me a prize *I* like than a horrible platter all over rosebuds? Please, Dicky! Please! You promise me you 'll win *this* one. I want it."

Meredith's gesture was negative, but not impatient.

" But, Eleanor, I 'm not joking; I 'm serious. You don't know the first thing about tournaments, do you? So you 'll have to take my word for it; golf is n't that sort of game. Everybody does his best, and takes what comes to him. I —"

" But it 's only a *game,* is n't it? " Her emphasis was pregnant.

" Yes — and no."

" Then I should think," said Miss Winsted, judgmatically, " that if you have all the fun of playing, and if you 're so anxious to call this an engagement present, you 'd *want* to let me have my card-tray."

" But — you see, it 's like this: you qualify, and then —"

" If you won't do that much for me," she grieved, " I don't see how you can pretend to love me so *very* well. And I 've set my heart on that tray! "

Meredith gasped. He perceived now that a casual explanation would n't do; Miss Winsted required elementary education. An endeavor to convince her at this juncture, while their relationship was so new, must inevitably lead to misfortune. She was so incredibly naïve, so wholly unfamiliar with the facts, they might even quarrel. Meredith shivered at the mere imagining of it. Besides, what was the St. Valentine's in comparison with matrimony? He had been longing to demonstrate his love for her; could there be a greater renunciation than this? Could there be loftier heroism than to slay his ambitions for her sake? And later, when she had come to understand what he had done for her, would she ever forget it? Meredith swallowed hard. Then a flood of pity and of altruistic ardor swept over him, and he had his initial taste of the bitter-sweet of solemn sacrifice. Golf! Faugh! She loved him! He smiled bravely at her, and she clutched his arm and pressed it excitedly.

" You will, won't you, Dicky? "

" Anything you want," said Meredith, deliberately, " I 'll get for you, or break something trying. Let 's go in and dance."

As they moved from the table he could console himself only by the recollection that if he had n't come to Pinehurst, he would n't have met Miss Winsted. Simultaneously with his oblique promise, he regretted that he had given it; but as he contemplated her joy, he did n't dare to retract. Sorrowfully, as they passed down the long corridor to the ball-room, he wondered what sort of prizes had been purchased for the Spring tournament. As far as the St. Valentine's was concerned, he was a renegade, and he had sold his birthright.

On the first tee of the championship course Meredith and his qualifying partner, a Sleepy Hollow crack named Scott, waited for the pair in front to advance beyond the white stake which marked the safety zone. Meredith had n't slept well: he was depressed and enervated, and, to his further discomfiture, he was acutely aware of the gallery; he felt that he was being eyed suspiciously, and that people would detect his ruse and misconstrue it, and call him a mug-hunter. But Eleanor wanted that tray; she couldn't see why she shouldn't have it, and Meredith was Penthesilean. He had essayed feebly to convert her to his point of view, and failing, he had sworn her never to mention the incident to a soul, and in perplexed loyalty she had consented. He was a conspirator, but he was safe from indictment. He prodded the ground with the driving-iron he had elected to use for the get-away, and rolled his wrists to ascertain their suppleness.

"How's your game?" he inquired of Scott. "What'd you do yesterday?"

"A sloppy eighty."

"Eighty doesn't sound hopelessly sloppy to me."

"It was, though. I had all the breaks. You've been doing very well, haven't you?"

"I'm erratic," lied Meredith. "Best I expect is the second flight."

"Piffle!" said Scott. "You'll have to be close to eighty-five. Don't talk nonsense!"

"Very in-and-out golf. They're clear now. Your honor."

He had decided to shoot expressly for an eighty-seven, which should land him comfortably in the lower half of the second division; and to furnish the public with a visible reason for this figure, he had plotted out a campaign based on the peculiarities of the course itself. All he needed was a little wildness from the tees, and the sympathy of many friends would be spontaneous. So, after Scott had driven a low ball straight down the course, he began his meretricious policy by intentionally hooking into the first of many traps, and by playing from the hazard to the green with all the cunning at his command. Through this procedure, which should enable him to secure a consistent average of one over par, he acquired a six, which was his desire, on the first hole.

"Tough luck!" said Scott. "Lots more holes, though."

"I'll straighten 'em out," predicted Meredith, hooking carefully from the second tee. "I'm working to counteract a slice."

He played faultlessly from the rough to the cup, and took his five, one over par; but as he stepped back, to remove his shadow from Scott's line of vision, he was suddenly overcome by a revulsion of feeling which sickened him. He was purposely failing to play his best; he was meticulously designing to place himself in a division where he didn't belong; after winning three easy matches he was to stultify himself by throwing away the finals in order that Miss Winsted might have her card-tray! It was unbelievable. It was n't within the bounds of sanity. It was n't golf, and not for all the women in the world could he become a traitor to his sportsmanship. He would n't go on with the farce; he would n't!

" Your shot, Dick. Down the alley this time, now! "

Meredith, with his mind in the club-house, topped dismally among the wiry grasses. He attempted a recovery, but the ball, slewing to the left, sought lodgment in a deep heel-print. His third ran swiftly to a cavernous trap, and bobbed against the embankment.

" You looked up," his partner accused him.

" That," said Meredith, wide-eyed, " is what Grant Rice calls the ' Tragedy of the Hoisted Bean.' Well, I deserved it."

Niblick in hand, he descended to the depths of the pit. The ball was virtually unplayable; it had dropped into a crevice formed by the face of the trap, and by a bushel or two of sand which had poured down from it in a miniature avalanche. Meredith studied the lie and sighed prodigiously.

" I 'll have to waste enough shots to cut away the back of this cañon before I can reach the ball at all," he announced dolefully. " Well, it 's got to be done."

The sand was obdurate. Meredith, flailing vigorously, played four and five and six. His seventh shot was a masterpiece of destructive engineering; his eighth extricated him nicely; he was on in ten and down in an exact dozen, and his score for the first three holes was twenty-three. Yesterday he had played them for a total of thirteen.

" Too bad! Darned tough luck!" said Scott. " I never saw a worse lie than that in my life. It was impossible."

Meredith, who in his absorption had forgotten all about the hypocrisy to which he had consecrated this round, grinned broadly. His ill fate operated as a release from his hated penance; he was free!

" Got 'em all out of my cosmos now," he declared. " Here goes for that eighty-five."

" Hope you make it; but you 'll have to shoot close to even fours, old top."

" Bet you a box of balls I 'm eighty-seven or better," offered Meredith, rashly.

" Take you!" said Scott. " And I don't care if I lose. Double it?"

" *Right!* " said Meredith. He whaled out a terrific drive, pitched an approach to a green on which an inept pitch is fatal, and took a four when one more oscillation of the sphere would have given him a birdie three. " I expect to turn," said Meredith, brightly, " in a snappy forty-six."

" With a twelve in it? I 've got another box of balls that says you 're an incorrigible optimist."

" You 're on," agreed Meredith. " Do these balls break if you hit 'em too hard? "

His heart was singing now, and his mood was exalted. Two strokes, no more, he had intentionally tossed away. His drive from the third tee had gone wrong through no intent of his own; his troubles in the pit had been fortuitous. All those tremendous efforts at extrication had been honest, sturdy efforts. He had discounted his intelligence only by the first two tee-shots; he had been legitimately penalized; he would have to play flawless golf to qualify even in the second flight. All his depression had vanished; he felt no longer enervated; he was alert, and keen, and daring, and he could play the best that was in him.

" Beau-tiful drive! " said Scott.

" I 'll begin to land on 'em in a minute," promised Meredith, stoutly. " There 's another twenty yards to those if I can ever connect."

He did n't turn in forty-six,— he was forty-seven,— but it was a gross indentation of the sand of the ninth green which robbed him of his par three. For six successive holes he had played to the card; he was indubitably certain that he could come in under forty; he would have both the satisfaction of good golf and of Miss Winsted's praise; the Furies were kind to him. For the first seven of the in-holes he took only thirty strokes, and as he drove with a jigger on the short seventeenth, he told himself that his eighty-five was assured. Whereupon the ball veered inconsiderately to the left, and burrowed into the finely granulated floor of the farther trap.

It took him five for that hole, and four for the eighteenth, and he was gratified not only by the mathematics of the medal round, but also because he had netted a box of balls from Scott. He hurried to the second floor of the club-house and scanned the score-board; noted that already a respectable number of high seventies and low eighties had been recorded, and dashed back to the hotel to join Miss Winsted. They lunched together in the utmost harmony, they sat together on the veranda afterward, they were amicably agreeing that Westchester cottages possess inherent advantages over Riverside Drive apartments, when a boy summoned Meredith to the telephone. When he emerged he was apologetic.

" What is it? " he queried.

" More golf," said Meredith, sheepishly.

Miss Winsted was mildly offended.

" But you *told* me you didn't have to go out again until to-morrow —"

" Unfortunately," said Meredith, "everybody shot the same sort of game to-day. The low score in the second flight was an eighty-four, and the highest was an eighty-six. Five of us tied for three places. I've got to go over for the play-off."

" I'll come with you," said Miss Winsted, rising promptly. " It counts for my tray, does n't it ? "

So that when the five tense golfers gathered for the combat which would eliminate two of their number, Meredith had the personal backing of the prettiest girl in Pinehurst, and he liked the consciousness of it, even although he knew that she was indifferent to all but the tangible token of his success.

He was the last to drive, and all of his predecessors had bungled. Meredith smiled as he swung his weighted iron. The hole was a par five, but barely over the 425-yard limit. On innumerable occasions he had made it in four, but in a play-off in which two men out of five were slated for defeat, he realized that the higher figure would unquestionably be good enough to insure him his place. He therefore spared the iron, and, to his horror, sliced execrably into the woods.

During his younger days he had often known the exquisite agony of playing the decisive hole against grave odds. He had accomplished his share of victories under these conditions, he had met with his share of downfalls. Yesterday he had dreamed of triumph after triumph; now, as he located his ball nestling at the trunk of a small tree, he was hot with anger and resentment. He, a man with a seventy-four over the No. 2 course on Monday, was playing on Tuesday to break a tie for last place in an inferior division, and his was the worst of five inglorious drives! And what a fool he'd look if he went down to the third flight!

He could get no easy stance, and the tree prevented him from even a quarter swing. He had to chop the ball, and although he sent it skipping clear from the pine-grove, he was still in the rough and in the most irritating of strategic positions. He played three, and he played four; he was ten good yards from the green, and the other four balls were well on.

" How many? " he inquired of the field in general.

" Four."

" Three here."

" I'm four, too."

" I lie four."

"CONSOLATION"

Meredith scowled. If he played safely, he had a sure six; but two of the other men were dead to the hole, one had a six-foot putt, and the most distant ball belonged to the player who was on in three. There was a certainty, then, that Meredith could hope for nothing better than a miscue by one of those who lay dead. The six-foot putt, if missed, would result in at least a six, and two sixes would thereby be scored against three potential fives. There was n't one chance in a million, however, that either of the men who lay dead would miscue. Neither would they be attacked by vertigo.

"In a play-off for the second sixteen," said Meredith, cynically, to himself, "I'll shoot for the hole!"

With a few other spectators, Miss Winsted was standing a few feet behind him. He knew that she was watching him attentively, but he did n't dare to turn his head. Three things must occupy his mind, the club, the ball, the hole. There was no room here for Miss Winsted. He sighted with his putter across the sandy soil and across the level surface of the green.

"Caddy," snapped Meredith, "take away the flag!"

He putted, and the ball never deviated from the line; it ran pleasantly to the zinc, and tinkled home.

The ball never deviated from the line; it ran pleasantly to the zinc, and tinkled home

"Down in five," said Meredith, rigidly controlling his facial muscles. The man with the six-foot putt straightway missed it, both the men who were dead missed theirs, the man who had been on in three was down in five, and seized Meredith's arm and beckoned to Miss Winsted.

"*We're* both in it," he proclaimed. "The other fellows have got to keep on playing. Wasn't that some shot of Dicky's from off the green, Miss Winsted?"

"I didn't see it," she conceded, squeezing Meredith's hand. "Did it count for my — *ouch!*" Meredith had squeezed back.

"How could you help seeing it?"

"Why, I was looking at that pickaninny with the flag," she said artlessly. "What was *he* doing?"

"Zowie!" choked their companion, and, being a gentleman, proceeded to enlighten her in detail.

But Meredith was thinking that he could probably teach her a great deal before the Spring tournament. He'd have to.

According to his reckoning, there were three days of bliss in store for him, three days in which he could extend himself as he liked without regard for the awful anticlimax to come. He cherished, to be sure, the hope that by Saturday he would succeed in coaching Miss Winsted so that she would be willing to let him win the ornate inkstand which was the secretary's trophy; but prior to that he could swamp three antagonists in a row, and right vengefully he sallied forth to swamp them. And Wednesday evening found him thankful to be a victor at the twentieth hole.

" Why, it was uncanny! " he related to the group in the locker-room. " I went out in thirty-six, and that ought to be good for *some*thing in Class B any day! This man Hendricks took forty-six, and I was *one down!* "

" It can't be done," said Scott. " Who's got an adding-machine? "

" Well, it *was*. He had two par holes, three birdies, and Heaven knows how many shots on the other holes! About eleven apiece! You never saw such a match-play round in your life. Then I went all to pieces, and took forty-five to come home; he got a forty, and we were all square. It was the same thing, only reversed. I had all threes, fours, and sevens. We halved the first extra hole in three — two eagles! I was on in two, and took one putt, and he holed out a full mashie! Then he went up in the air a mile. The twentieth I won in four to eight. We were both on in three, and I took one putt to his five. *Some* golf! "

" You'll have your hands full to-morrow," prophesied Scott. " Wilson's an old war-horse. Look out for him!"

" With both eyes wide open," said Meredith, departing.

He departed to search for Miss Winsted, and found her on a bench overlooking the trio of practice-greens. She was leaning slightly forward, so that her attitude was suggestive of rather studious contemplation; and as she made room for Meredith, she motioned in the direction of two ancient devotees who were squabbling over half-stymies.

" I think I could do that," she remarked. " As well as they can, anyhow."

" Let's see," exclaimed Meredith, his heart pounding. " You wait here a second!"

He was back in a jiffy, equipped with a hitherto unused putter and a pocketful of brand-new balls. He wasn't going to detract from Miss Winsted's timid enthusiasm by furnishing second-hand implements.

" There," he said, " try a couple. Oh, not so far away! Stand about here. Now hold it the way I do."

Miss Winsted putted clear across the sand, across the adjoining green, and out into the roadway.

" Let me try another, Dicky," she demanded, coloring.

" Not so hard," he admonished. " Remember, it's only about ten feet. Swing like this. I want you to feel the club."

Miss Winsted putted eight inches.

" We'll go a little nearer, dear. That's fine. Now putt!"

Miss Winsted obediently shoved the ball, and pushed it into the hole. The blade of the putter descended with it and jammed. Miss Winsted was outspokenly delighted.

" But you must n't push it," expostulated Meredith. " See, like this."

" Like this?" Miss Winsted smote the ball sixty feet toward the club-house, and was suffused with shame.

" Once more, dear."

She grasped the club firmly, and focused upon the hole with great ferocity.

" This time," she said, " I'll put it in."

She did. From four feet she holed out in four shots. And then because people were calling to her from the veranda, and rallying her, she defaulted.

" I'm embarrassed now," she said confidentially to Meredith; " but you come out with me when there's nobody looking — Really, Dicky, it is n't so *awfully* simple, is it? I thought it was so easy it was childish!"

"You follow us part way round to-morrow," he proposed, animated by an unholy joy, "and see what golf really looks like. Will you?"

"Well, if you 'll promise to win my tray for me."

Meredith coughed. For the moment he had n't been thinking of the disgrace scheduled for Saturday.

"You watch me!" he said with meaning ambiguity.

On Thursday Meredith met the type of golfer who never plays under eighty or over ninety, the hardest possible opponent for a nervous man to beat. And Meredith was nervous, largely because he felt that Miss Winsted, who was following the match, would judge him and judge the game by her first impressions. He was two down at the ninth, and there she announced that she was tired and thought she 'd go back; whereupon, Meredith, freed from his inhibitions, proceeded to win his match four up and three to go. The old war-horse stated in the locker-room that Meredith had played the second half of the course in one under fours, but this was naturally taken as a slight exaggeration devised

335

to show that the old war-horse himself had been playing respectable golf.

On Friday Meredith awoke to find that a typical Pinehurst cold wave had crept upon them in the night and that the thermometer was perilously low. Moreover, a ghastly wind was cutting across the plateau, offering no solace and threatening dire punishment to those who had to face it. He went out in the expectation of being chilled to the bone, and although he wore two sweaters in addition to his Norfolk jacket, he was duly confirmed in his opinion. He went after his man brutally, piled up a lead of five holes, with seven to go, and suddenly succumbed to the knife-edged wind. He had lost a bit of his lead, but he was n't worrying about it until it occurred to him that this was really the crucial match; he must necessarily win it in order to lose to-morrow. Distraught by this requirement, perturbed by the regularity with which his knees were knocking together, and tormented with doubt because his hands were rapidly growing too numb to hold the clubs, he plowed along to the seventeenth without once getting the ball off the ground. By that time the match was all square, and his antagonist was colder than Meredith. Consequently, the last hole was a classic.

Sears, a gaunt slasher from Dunwoodie, began by

hitting a good foot behind the ball in his haste to get the shot over with and his hands back in his pockets. Subsequently he batted a lumbering grounder into the rough, and retired behind his caddy to warm his face. Meredith's driver twisted in his grip so that he caught the ball squarely with the toe of it, and achieved a rod and a half. On his second endeavor, when frosty tears were running down his cheeks, and all his fingers were stiff and wooden, he missed the ball completely; but Sears was clawing his road to the fairway, and polluting the atmosphere with fervid expletives. Side by side they pushed on past the yawning trap; Meredith reached the green in five to Sears's six; both took two putts and broke for the club-house without lingering in the open air for any handshaking formalities that could be fully as well performed in front of an open fire. But Meredith had gained the finals, and the card-tray was Miss Winsted's if he chose to take it for her.

That night he told her explicitly just what she had asked of him and what he had done.

" Maybe," he said, " you could n't understand it before, because you could n't visualize the situation, dear. But now I 'm in the finals. I can get your tray for you without going out of the hotel. All I need to do is to default, and that would be what

337

men call 'yellow.' Or I can go out and lose deliberately. Well, suppose I do. I'll simply have deprived somebody else of a privilege that I don't want. I'll have acted like a dog in a manger. And more than that, it isn't really fair. I do hope you'll understand. It isn't the material trophies we're playing for —"

"I think I do understand now," she granted quickly. "I've been awfully silly, Dicky. It didn't mean anything at all to me; I thought it was quite all right. I *do* see now, though, because I'm getting interested. Here you ought to have been in a higher class —"

Meredith shook his head.

"I've been mighty glad," he said, "that after I blew those two strokes in the qualifying round I did get into a mess. Even if I'd started out well, I couldn't have beaten eighty-four, and that would have put me in the second flight, anyway. Those two strokes were all I blew. So my conscience doesn't hurt me the least bit in the world. The only thing is about to-morrow."

Miss Winsted rose, and led him to the table where the prizes were displayed.

"If you win from Mr. Osborne," she inquired, "you'll get that inkstand?" She pointed to a decorative utility which would have charmed an Elk; it had everything on it but hoofs.

" I 'm afraid I will," said Meredith. " It certainly is a he-inkstand, is n't it? "

Miss Winsted bestowed a final look of farewell upon the plain little tray she had coveted. As for the inkstand, she could n't remotely imagine it in her own room or anywhere in her house; it properly belonged on a huge desk in a hunting lodge. But, after all, it had an inner significance which formerly had escaped her. In any event, Meredith would merely be complying with the usual custom if he bought her an engagement gift instead of winning one.

" You play the best you can," she said impulsively. " I don't care if it 's for a platter or an inkstand or an egg-cup, you do your best, Dicky! " And it was with that resolve, and in the loftiest of moods, that he approached his ultimate match on Saturday morning.

The weather had moderated, and the day was clear and balmy. A brief rain at midnight had put the greens in superb condition; a warm sun had added the precise degree of crispness that Pinehurst turf demands; there could n't have been a finer morning on which to live or to play a round of golf.

Meredith was in ecstasy; he cared less for golf to-day than he did for living; he was so thoroughly imbued with the spirit of the fraternity of man that he hoped for Osborne almost as much as he hoped for himself. On a day like this, what difference did it make who won or lost? They could play golf.

But after Osborne had drawn first blood, Meredith's temper changed, and he was very ready to dispose of his excess of vivacity. By another hole or two he recognized the fact that he was playing against a man who also was worthy of the championship division. Instead of resorting to strange expedients in order to lose, he must force himself to the extreme in order to win. His eyes brightened, and he set courageously about his task.

In the competition of two men like these there is, as Henry Leach has said, at least one element in common with the prize-ring. Each stroke is a direct attack upon the opponent's poise. Each shot has not only a purpose in itself; it also aims to produce a definite effect upon the adversary. It is a species of moral assault and battery, a duel of nerves and reflexes. And Osborne and Meredith, both students of the game and craftsmen of it, fought to the ninth on even terms.

It was at the tenth hole that Meredith's luck deluded him. He had driven far over the pond hazard and up the hill, and his second shot was a scant yard from the cup. Osborne, playing logically, went for the hole, and overran, got down in four, and stood apart, communing with the gods. Meredith had privately set down his three; he played mechanically, and for an instant he thought, so concentrated had he been upon the stroke, that he had holed. Osborne exclaimed sharply. The ball was hanging over the cavity so near the edge that it seemed continuously in the act of falling. A three-foot putt, and Meredith had n't given it a chance! He had squandered a hole, he had thrown away a golden opportunity!

" A half," he said, affecting a smile.

" You deserve to win it," claimed Osborne, generously.

" I 'll go after you on the next one," laughed Meredith, scourging himself.

The eleventh hole was a lusty four hundred yards and over; Osborne was short on his second, and Meredith was hole high. Both ran up well, Osborne was away, and negotiated a par four without a tremor.

" This for a half," said Meredith, gaging the distance.

He was warning himself not to repeat the error of putting too softly; and as he made the injunction permanent, he recalled Miss Winsted's grotesque attempt on the practice green, when she had sent her ball traveling out to the roadway. It may have been this image which misled him, for his shot was too powerful by the slightest of margins; the ball struck the back of the cup and bounded over by an inch or two, and Meredith groaned inwardly with astonishment and chagrin.

"Your hole," he granted, crushing down his wrath.

"Too bad!" sympathized Osborne. "You're beating yourself; *I*'m not."

They halved the twelfth, but on the next hole Meredith had another terrible putt of a yard, and went into a fit of the fidgets. Once he had overplayed from this distance, once he had underplayed; this time he would be trebly sure. He surveyed the line, and swung the putter with great care. If the line had been straight, Meredith would have had his half; as it was, the ball paused opposite the center of the hole, a bare inch to the right.

"Two down," he said, stooping, "and six to go. Still your honor."

On the fourteenth he missed a seven-footer for a four, and got a half in five. Utter demoralization on the greens had seized him; he was two down, with four to play, and if he could have had what

any golfer would be pleased to call his just deserts,
he would have been dormie. But Osborne was in
trouble on the 212-yard fifteenth, and Meredith had
no mercy.

" Now for the inkstand," he told himself on the
tee.

He had chosen a spoon, and he played it impec-
cably. He was reflecting that the match would be
decided not by what Osborne did, but what Meredith did; and after he had construed the wild ges-
ticulations of the caddy ahead, he was aware that he
had made the green, and held it. He was wholly
callous to Osborne's splendid pitch from the rough;
he was rather contemptuous of it. After all, what
was the profit in winning or losing the second flight?
In one case, a transient pleasure and a desultory
series of congratulations; in the other, a silver card-
tray for a pretty girl who did n't know a brassey
from a maul-stick.

" Oh, rubbish!" said Meredith to himself as he
nonchalantly holed a prodigious putt for a two.
Aloud he stated, " You 're one up and three to play,
Mr. Osborne."

They halved the sixteenth after a heart-breaking
struggle; at the 165-yard seventeenth Meredith saw
that Miss Winsted had wandered over from the
club-house, and was watching them from the shade

of the trees near the green. He gazed at her for a moment, and turned to Osborne.

"Now, as man to man," said Meredith, bluntly, "I want to know what you think of that ink-pot we're shooting for? Honestly."

Osborne, somewhat taken aback, grinned widely.

"Hideous thing, is n't it?"

"Suppose you win it," said Meredith, teeing his ball, "what'll you do with it?"

"Hide it, I suppose. Funny game, is n't it? Two of us breaking our necks for something neither of us wants. But my wife would give her soul for that dinky little tray they've put up for the second prize."

Meredith grimaced.

"She would, would she?"

"Absolutely. She's mad about it."

Meredith glanced at the green.

"Well, you'll have to hole out to beat me, Mr. Osborne."

"I usually do from here." Both laughed.

Meredith drove, and was on; and Osborne, after deep cogitation, played a careful shot to the very boundary of the green. Abreast they marched through the intervening rough.

"I almost hope you win," said Meredith, absently. "I don't want that ink-stand."

344

" Neither do I; but I 'm doing my darndest to take it away from you, don't you think? "

" You 've got *me* working. But it looks as though I 've got the edge on you here."

" Hardly," said Osborne, with charming friendliness. " I 'll halve this with you and win the last, two up! "

" Shoot from there! " commanded Meredith.

Osborne shot, and went dead. Meredith bent over his putter, and then stood erect.

" It 's a funny game," he repeated, " the funniest game in the world. Vardon was right; he says it 's an *awful* game. I think I must believe in foreordination. I 'd bet a hundred to one this goes down! And we 're playing for a piece of junk neither of us would have in the house if it did n't represent this match, and we 're both set on winning it! A hundred to one! " He putted, and never a ball rolled straighter to its goal. " A two to your three," he remarked to the stupefied Osborne. " All square, and one to go. Just a second."

He walked over to Miss Winsted and patted her arm affectionately.

" Are you ahead of him? " she asked, with anxiety.

" We 're all even so far."

" You 'll win, won't you? "

"Is that what you want? I came over to find out."

"I do, dear; I *do!* And — I thought you'd like to know — I — I took a lesson from Peacock this morning!"

"You *did!*" cried Meredith, astounded. "You *did!* Well, you just wait until I win this hole, and see what you get!"

Transported, he drove magnificently, and Osborne was alongside. With inexpressible rapture, he played perfectly between the twin traps guarding the green, and Osborne was with him. He ran an approach within a precious yard of the hole, and Osborne was a foot farther away. And Osborne, too deliberate to be accurate, missed the hole by a hand's-breadth.

"I'll give you that for a five," proffered Meredith. "And I'm playing four — for the hole and match."

"It looks like your inkstand," admitted Osborne, whitening, although his lips were curving. "You ought to fill it with champagne."

Meredith nodded appreciatively, and took his putter. Miss Winsted was again behind him, and he felt her presence, and welcomed it. She'd taken a lesson, had she? She was adopting the game because he loved it, was she? He owed her something for that — something more than ordinary gratitude. And now that she had come to share his laurels with him, she should see at least that golf is more than a simple game played for prizes; she should see that it is a cross-section of life, played for whatever reward is decreed. The rule is to play hard, and take the consequences. His jaw tightened, and he shook off a fantasy which had crept upon him, a fleeting notion to shut his eyes as he played, and to make Miss Winsted a gift of his pride and of her card-tray. He frowned, and dismissed the sordid conception. Love is love, but golf is golf, and Meredith had a simple putt for the win. He was sorry for Osborne, but the match and the inkstand belonged to him. Osborne's wife would be jubilant, and Miss Winsted would some day fathom the mystery of the game, and be hedonic, too. He addressed the ball; and whimsically a picture of the unsuitable prize rose before him, and a chuckle died in his throat. And then, paralyzed, staggered by the egregious fault he had committed, he straightened himself, and looked at Osborne.

"What's up?"

"I touched it!" said Meredith, thickly.

"Go on! This is a gentleman's game."

"This is *golf*," corrected Meredith. "I touched it, and it moved."

" You can't waive it. That's mighty decent of
you, but it's against the rules. I'm playing five,
for a half."

" Oh, look here —"

" It's all right," said Meredith, gnawing his lip.
" *You* did n't make the rules, I ought to have had
more sense."

" Here, you forget it —"

" Playing five," said Meredith, sternly. " I may
halve it yet."

" Well, I hope you do. Take your time —"

" Drop!" breathed Meredith to the ball, and
missed the half by an eyelash. Osborne had beaten
him one up.

Late that afternoon he went with Miss Winsted
to the table loaded with silverware, removed the
card-tray, and presented it to her with unction.

" It's yours, dear," he said; " but if I'd kept my
wits about me —"

" Mr. Osborne's told *everybody* about it," she
said quietly. " He says he would n't have known
about your touching your ball if you had n't told
him yourself; and even if you did n't win; it's a
consolation to know you lost like that, is n't it?
By penalizing yourself when you need n't have —"

" Also," said Meredith not too truthfully, " to

give you the present you picked out. And to have you take up golf as a result of this tournament. I 'll remember it always." He remained staring into vacancy until Miss Winsted pinched his elbow and brought him back to earth.

"What *are* you thinking about?" she demanded.

"Oh — nothing," said Meredith, averting his face. "I was just wondering whether you 'd better take lessons of Peacock or Alec Ross." Once more he had spoken falsely; he had been thinking about the Spring tournament, and the feebleness of his short game to-day. And then the real consolation came warmly over him, and he was placid and content. "Let 's go out while it 's light enough," he said, "and practise our putting together. Want to?"

He had won companionship.

THE END

349

CPSIA information can be obtained at www.ICGtesting.com
Printed in the USA
BVOW052338131112

305470BV00004B/5/P

9 781148 002538